ROUTLEDGE LIBRARY EDITIONS: SOCIAL THEORY

Volume 50

THE PERSON IN THE SIGHT OF SOCIOLOGY

THE PERSON IN THE SIGHT OF SOCIOLOGY

COLIN FLETCHER

LONDON AND NEW YORK

First published in 1975

This edition first published in 2015
by Routledge
2 Park Square, Milton Park, Abingdon, Oxon, OX14 4RN

and by Routledge
711 Third Avenue, New York, NY 10017

Routledge is an imprint of the Taylor & Francis Group, an informa business

First issued in paperback 2016

© 1975 Colin Fletcher

All rights reserved. No part of this book may be reprinted or reproduced or utilised in any form or by any electronic, mechanical, or other means, now known or hereafter invented, including photocopying and recording, or in any information storage or retrieval system, without permission in writing from the publishers.

Trademark notice: Product or corporate names may be trademarks or registered trademarks, and are used only for identification and explanation without intent to infringe.

British Library Cataloguing in Publication Data
A catalogue record for this book is available from the British Library

ISBN13: 978-1-138-78810-7 (hbk)
ISBN13: 978-1-138-99801-8 (pbk)

Publisher's Note
The publisher has gone to great lengths to ensure the quality of this reprint but points out that some imperfections in the original copies may be apparent.

Disclaimer
The publisher has made every effort to trace copyright holders and would welcome correspondence from those they have been unable to trace.

Colin Fletcher

The person in the sight of sociology

Routledge & Kegan Paul
London and Boston

First published in 1975
by Routledge & Kegan Paul Ltd
Broadway House, 68-74 Carter Lane,
London EC4V 5EL and
9 Park Street,
Boston, Mass. 02108, USA
Set in IBM Century 10 on 13 point
and printed in Great Britain by Lowe & Brydone
(Printers) Ltd., Thetford, Norfolk
© Colin Fletcher 1975
No part of this book may be reproduced in
any form without permission from the
publisher, except for the quotation of brief
passages in criticism
ISBN 0 7100 8119 7 (c)
   0 7100 8120 0 (p)

THE PERSON IN THE SIGHT OF SOCIOLOGY

COLIN FLETCHER

LONDON AND NEW YORK

First published in 1975

This edition first published in 2015
by Routledge
2 Park Square, Milton Park, Abingdon, Oxon, OX14 4RN

and by Routledge
711 Third Avenue, New York, NY 10017

Routledge is an imprint of the Taylor & Francis Group, an informa business

First issued in paperback 2016

© 1975 Colin Fletcher

All rights reserved. No part of this book may be reprinted or reproduced or utilised in any form or by any electronic, mechanical, or other means, now known or hereafter invented, including photocopying and recording, or in any information storage or retrieval system, without permission in writing from the publishers.

Trademark notice: Product or corporate names may be trademarks or registered trademarks, and are used only for identification and explanation without intent to infringe.

British Library Cataloguing in Publication Data
A catalogue record for this book is available from the British Library

ISBN13: 978-1-138-78810-7 (hbk)
ISBN13: 978-1-138-99801-8 (pbk)

Publisher's Note
The publisher has gone to great lengths to ensure the quality of this reprint but points out that some imperfections in the original copies may be apparent.

Disclaimer
The publisher has made every effort to trace copyright holders and would welcome correspondence from those they have been unable to trace.

For my Mother —
that she may know where I have been

Contents

Acknowledgments	ix
1 Sighting the person	1
2 A theory of the person	13
3 The cup of constants	24
4 The plain of contradictions	38
5 The wheel of the life-cycle	52
6 Some thoughts which may be obvious	64
7 Sociology in the light of the person	74
Annotations	83
Bibliography	91

Acknowledgments

I wrote this essay as a direct response to Dr Diana Leat's question, 'But what is a person? Who are you talking about?' I had reached the point of apoplexy during a seminar wherein people were patients and reduced to ciphers accordingly.

Lyn, my wife, loved me whilst I wrote out this essay. John Parker thought it had guts.

Then I left all I had written and tried to 'test' the ideas in life. And here I acknowledge the help of those whose struggles I have shared in these last three years.

Tentatively I submitted my scruffy jottings to Peter Hopkins and without his encouragement they would have been shapeless to this day. K.E. Morgan has been the source of many strengths during this later exercise.

Grace Pearce has typed so willingly that I now feel sure of saying something even if I am still not fully sure of what I say.

But, in conclusion, I should thank God and man and the times in which we live. Is it still possible for truth and naiveté to be so close?

1

Sighting the person

Making a start

'Problems of the nature of human nature are raised most urgently when the life-routines of a society are disturbed, when men are alienated from their social roles in such a way as to open themselves up for new insight. When social affairs proceed smoothly "human nature" seems to fit so neatly into traditional routines that no general problem is presented; men know what to expect from one another; their vocabularies for various emotions and their stereotyped motives are taken for granted and seem common to all. But when society is in deep-going transformation and men are pivots of historic change, they challenge one another's explanations of conduct, and human nature itself becomes problematic.'

Gerth and Mills (1954: xvii)

Sociology is not just about the development of society it is about the context of the person's development.

'Man is a focus not merely of levels or dimensions but also of polarities of antithetical attitudes, principles or values. All things are characterised by both change and constancy, all realities exemplify both unity and plurality, both mediacy and immediacy, both identity and difference.'

Mukerjee (1961:15)

֍

Man has soul. This is a religious statement because it uses a religious concept. But even though man is 'abandoned' (Sartre 1945), there is more to his life than five senses and few simple drives. There are forces that he respects and musters to enable action. These forces do not holistically make soul. Holistically, though the forces are distinct, separable and related, they do not make the person. A force is not 'free conscious activity'.

The person is an ideal universal and to that indestructible property we take for finite life we attribute soul.

֍

Sociology was the study and reconciliation of the citizen and the nation state in advanced capitalist societies. It is unlikely to survive intact let alone develop in the current times of internationalism and socialism.

֍

The person cries out for beauty: for a structure which conceals nothing.

֍

Praxiology in late capitalist states is a thread of metaphysical humanism or social idealism. It is impractical except as to the insistence on how we see one another in encouraging, enabling and enveloping ways.

3 Sighting the person

⑨

Equilibrium is not possible. There is always moment and momentum for which there is no balance in man. At no time has he arrived. At no time is he stable. He can be momentarily secure in the whirlwind or at its eye. But the 'balanced man' is an impossibility.

⑨

The crisis in sociology, that it has been benighted with sponsored tunnelling, has produced four alternatives for its young practitioners: social policy; retreats to philosophy and history; obsessions with methodologies and committed journalism.

⑨

'Much of any man's effort to know the social world around him is prompted by an effort, more or less disguised or deliberate, to know things as they are personally important to him; which is to say he aims at knowing himself and the experiences he has had in his social world (his relationship to it) and at *changing* this relationship in some manner.'
Gouldner (1969: 41)

⑨

It is not how do you hang on but why? The person has a reason for his sanity or his unreasonableness is the early warning of his path to insanity.

⑨

'What Marx is saying is that because I have eyes I have the need to see; because I have ears I have the need to hear;

4 Sighting the person

because I have a brain I have the need to think and because I have a heart I have the need to feel. In short, because I am a man, I am in need of man and of the world.'

Fromm (1968: 10)

Psychology may draw upon abnormality but sociology is the study for the universalization of sanity — the problem being should a single person go/be mad?[1]

℘

The person is perfect.
What everyone?
Yes everyone — even thee and me.
Really perfect?
Yes perfectible, perfecting and perfect.

A loud confession

I write of an ideal: a person who is pure, harmonious and fulfilling.
   This may be too sweet for jaded palettes.
   I wish to note that the person is perfect as a necessary political act and corrective, and because it is only with this unequivocal assumption that we can proceed to see our nation states as oppressive.
   I have used a personal dogmatism and optimism to produce my effects. Many others have put the boot in on the prick-pulling, balls-cutting owner-bastards that run this country into the faces of its people. I leave it to you to decide what is actually wrong. I write of why it is legitimate, necessary and compulsory to love oneself and others.
   I write for my people — the young half-seeing; despairing generation.

5   Sighting the person

I write for sociologists of my generation (and the breakaway sages whom we respect) that we might work out our opposition to our culture and structure in terms of their inhumanity.

I also write to make a bench-mark of personal demystifications — not of my schooling but of what my miseducation shaped.

The true science of man is utopian: to say what man is — not of his needs but of his capabilities and of that which bleeds beneath his shackles.

Sociology needs an ontology which, perhaps unfortunately, cannot be culled from another discipline.

'Contemporary attempts to create a social science would (also) lead to a successful issue as the result of a little more precision. It should be founded upon the Platonic notion of the enormous animal, or the apocalytic notion of the Beast. Social science is the study of the enormous animal and should undertake a minute description of its anatomy, physiology, natural and conditional reflexes, capacity for being broken in.'[2]

Weil (1952: 280)

⑤

'Person: A self conscious being capable of choosing between alternative modes of behaviour on the basis of reflection. The person as a unit of sociological analysis is a social object, has a particular STATUS and performs social roles involving responsibilities to himself and others as a member of society and participant in its cultural ideas and traditions.'

Theodorson and Theodorson (1970: 296)

But can man be an 'object', albeit a 'social' one? Of course not! Or if he can it is because he has *statuses* and inhabits *roles* and we return to the real rubbish that passes for sociological work.

6   Sighting the person

'I am not here objecting to the use of mechanical or biological analogies as such, nor indeed to the intentional aspect of seeing man as a complex machine or animal. My thesis is limited to the contention that the theory of man as a person loses its way if it falls into an account of man as a machine or man as an organismic system of processes.'

Laing (1960: 22-3)

Freud did not think much of man. He thought the mind a fascinating labyrinth to explore for exploration's sake. The caves and tunnels were not much in themselves.

'Freud's psychology is a psychology of want. He defines pleasure as the satisfaction resulting from the removal of painful tensions. Phenomena of abundance, like love or tenderness, actually do not play any role in his system . . .

The sexual drive as a phenomenon of abundance, and sexual pleasure as spontaneous joy — the essence of which is not negative relief from tension — had no place in his psychology.'

Fromm (1942: 250-1)

A well-intentioned effort can be made, consciousness can be made the love of being:

'A person is not easily defined. The following outline, though it would not pass muster in a dictionary, captures roughly what I mean by the the term:

A person is a conscious being, one who thinks, feels and purposes, and carries these purposes into action, one who has active relationships with others — you can talk to a person and get a response, you can share feelings and ideas with him, argue with him; love him; hate him; you can know him in a way which can only be described as personal.'

France (1970: 26)

7 Sighting the person

Yet the sociological truth that the social being can only be known in a social context is missed. All ontologies isolate man. As if the commonsense individual were bits of mind and body grand or coward. Sociology can have nothing of this: man amongst men, personal properties are social products — a dynamic sociological psychology is called for that admits the true extent of relative drives in its subject.

⑤

A person is not an identity, or a role; or an actor or a persona or an incumbent. All of these terms take a part; they take apart. Mere representation is not enough. We can do more, we should know better, than to produce types of conformity.[3]

⑤

The 'term' stranger is one sociological representation of self and others.[4] It is the sociologist in circumstance, man in nature, man to man. It is an overpowering metaphor and a trap. The sociologist is not so distanced; he is not different in kind — his worries are certainly similar.

Nor is the person always odd. On occasions his problem is to establish a slight difference between himself and others that reassures his individuality. Should, then, a sociologist make an effort to reverse his direction — to turn again to the strangeness of the world?

This is all very well, but why insist on perfection?

Virtually all writers scorn the deification of man. Why, then, have I offended them with this elaborate construction? Why do I still find it acceptable? Or is it that without this exaggeration I cannot write on what is normal?

To tell of the person is to tell a story of him. To make the ideal type real the person is personified. I want to talk of him

— a man of ordinary innocence. For though we rant and rave over man's iniquities, his fall from grace and his bestial vices we know these to be obscenities by saying that man is not yet perfect.

Instead man, in our usual thinking, is forming, formed and accommodative. The worst we can say of man is that he gets used to his surroundings and in working his way out works those surroundings to the adequacy of a prison for himself. The worst we can say is that this realism acts to the detriment of vision and in working through situations man works himself into them.

⑤

The ideal *is* a distortion. It demands opinion by fact; belief by argument; faith by parody. The person is/was/shall be like this — but only as an idea.

⑤

The choice is to refuse to dwell upon a distortion. Many have become experts upon the dualism of the dubious. A unity has been found between lie and deception, saintliness and sycophancy, charm and cunning. If you would study deceit what is your purpose?

⑤

If, in sociology, the person has theoretical freedoms then his waywardness ceases to be the bane of prediction. The person is free to be with others; free to give and take; free to disappear and die.

Give the person his theoretical freedom, we might say, and his antics become actions, he is the author(ity) of his being.[5]

9 Sighting the person

'Our intuitive needs and feelings are still the best psychology we have.'

Hampden-Turner (1971: 179)

⑨

The answer to the question what is man is usually provided by some thoughts on the relationship between man and society. I assume that the notion of the person entails a being in a context. I take it as essential that this being is seen at the centre of his universe and that this world is not automatically either *the* society or *the* world.

The person is for his own purposes, and for mine, at the tranquil centre of turbulence.

The only reason for living is life. The energy that we use is a conversion of life material given purpose by our will. We make ourselves historical facts consuming and creating. Yet there is no neat cycle to this affair. There is no simple repetition. All that has happened is a basis for what is happening and what could happen. What could happen is not a problem but part of the problematic of past, present and future.

I know that I exist because I have an effect on others: to that extent I can see the quality of my own existence.[6]

The person is as a symphony resolved to a single note.

⑨

'It is the one great and universal interest of the human race to be cordially united and to aid each other to the fullest extent of their capabilities.'

Robert Owen's Tomb, Newtown

For all that your idea feels right; what is the sociological purpose of this concoction?

10   Sighting the person

'It seems to me that this is a variant of the theory of basic human needs which holds that certain social attributes of persons transcend specific cultural and historical contexts . . . Such a position, of course, runs counter to the mainstream of American sociology.'

Lehman (1973: 468)

☙

This essay on the person is substantively common-sense knowledge. Its facets are the taken for granted truths of those who have learned a little of survival. Though it may sound like a hymn, it is a song.[7] It is about the ordinary people's person.

☙

The big complaint has been that in all sociological modes man is an object. That in quantitative analysis he is a cipher, in qualitative analysis he is an actor and in Marxism he is a unit in a quite different reality.

☙

This essay is socio-analysis — the analysis of me in terms of you. The person does more than spill over into circumstance: he is given it and takes to it. There is a falsity in its presentation — it totalizes by property even if not by potential. This is more than a device, it is where I am up to. Socio-analysis begins with the self and relates to those who are normal.

☙

We do not judge the person's actions. We do not legislate beyond the Ten Commandments and the Beatitudes. The

11   Sighting the person

person is acting and creating or reacting and recreating. Administrative definitions of good and bad cannot be accepted, nor can notions of deviance.

Sociology is in part an apologia for the person and an apologetic for his enterprises from rebellion to movement. Sociology accepts the vitality of a change of heart.

☯

This thesis is a poor man's philosophy: that is it is sociological philosophy — it is an existential ontology for being with men. It is unlearned and meant to present the simplest of facts which sociology either witnesses or steamrolls into submission.

This is probably a premature attempt at sociological philosophy: a rounding upon the psychology of individuals that turns upon their situations. Consequently a concept is defined. The person is constructed by piecing together recent progressive knowledge to account for the drive in people and to argue for the liberation of the person.

☯

I cannot capture all experience. The subtleties, the nuances, the tinges of atmosphere in mirth, melodrama and absurdity — which some call bizarre — and the ways of men to freedom.

But do you think this sort of thinking does any good?

Creation and destruction are two principles of knowledge. The plan of the making of something is also a guide to its undoing. In drafting the properties or propensities of man as I understand them I have been acutely aware of the scheme's value for his control should it be correct. It may be that at this time making the 'whole' attracts more interest. But, what one generation has made another puts assunder with apparently equal reason. And it is no good anticipating abuse or even insisting that making is good whilst destruction is evil. No exercise of science or art can be made either foolproof or fiendproof.

Naturally I consider my own purposes as well-intentioned and the scheme I offer as 'leading to the good'. But I cannot assure anyone that it is either right or that it will never enable others to do wrong.

2

A theory of the person

> Human life is essentially, and not merely accidentally, social life. But once this is recognized, the concept of the individual as the ultimate social entity becomes questionable. If fundamentally man exists in terms and because of others who stand in reciprocal relation to him, then he is not ultimately determined by his primary indivisibility and singularity, but by the necessity of partaking of and communing with these others. This finds its expression in the concept of the person, no matter how vitiated by personalistic ethics and psychology this concept may be.
>
> Frankfurt Institute (1956: 40)

The person is a being. Further, the person is a moving part in sociological phenomena. In the sight of sociology the person is a part of life. For as this chapter's opening quotation says man exists with men.[1]

I now begin to unravel that which I think is personal. And I do so with a vision of there being parts to this whole. The whole I see as perfect.

Such 'parts' are properly understood as being no more than poetical devices. I deny that there are three parts in or to a person. The parts I categorize are means of understanding what is seen in the person, what is felt by the person and what is just as properly 'social'. I draw these parts about aspects of life which are either *constant* or *contradictory* or *cyclical*. In 'real terms' they are that which the person can do, is torn between and must do.

For example, a person can work, speak, embellish and believe. I call these 'constants'. As constants these faculties are work, language, art and cosmology. But I do not want you to memorize a list. Such properties are informed guesses. The statements made of them are true (in just this instant) in and around my life.

My word pictures can be easily dismissed. They could be true if you, yourself, catch reflections in a mirror. They could be true if you can see your way to making changes for the better. This conception of the person is not given to inspire any new approach to the subject matter of sociology; it is what sociological practitioners might expect to find at work.

My account of the characteristics of the person is not an account of motives. There is no suggestion that the person will say either this is what he is doing or this is why he wants to do it. Instead loosely-linked ideas have been used to overcome any degeneration into a debate on needs and motives.

In our time the most that can be said of motive is that the person does not 'want to be turned into some machine'.[2] Motives as an idea imply 'I want', 'I need': as if the person were a furnace demanding fuel. A searching, grabbing, consuming person does not exist. Such a person *would be* a machine.[3]

Instead the ideas of energy; imagination; will; capacity for strife and concern with struggle are used.[4] The tone of this description of the person claims that he is formless, forming and formed; embryonic, energetic and mature.

The construction of the person in this analysis is evident in the perspectives taken. First the person is fit and aware; well and intelligent; productive and benign. The person can do and think about doing. The person cannot do without

15 A theory of the person

thinking or think without doing. Body and mind are competent and co-operative. Second the person's outlook has both problems and potentials. The person sees the problem and realizes the potential. These assumptions are based on the 'natural'. The perspectives are the person's natural relationship with his contexts of thought and action. The perspectives articulate phenomena about the person — facts that are real inside and outside him.[5]

The metaphorical bases of the life-cycle, constants and contradictions

The life-cycle is a matter of necessity. For though life may be represented as a slowly revolving wheel each urge of this revolution is a surge of necessity. And though all may be necessity the surges are experienced as many, many, brief necessities.

Necessities emphasize physiology, organic realities of birth, growth, contraction, reproduction, death and decay. The metaphors for necessities are those of seed, season and cycle. The problem is going with such a movement; freedom within inexorable necessity; struggling to fullness and surviving instructed form. Necessities humble the person and inspire him to be as nature; to live a good life and to be glorious each moment of life. The person's necessity is to be a person; to have abundance, to know abundance, to create ever more abundance by continuous giving. Necessities make time for the person. The arc of his own time stretches backwards and forwards drawing upon his past, pointing his future. Necessities are the person's bond with nature; his nature, human nature and the world of nature. The potential is to be purposive, reproductive, restful to the pitch of peace.

Constants, in contrast, emphasize tangible relations; things, a material context. The realities are the properties of material: the resistance to shaping: the subtle strength of existing form.

16 A theory of the person

The metaphors for constants are those of stone and permanence. The problem is of being fixed by the material, locked within it, unable to confront it or change it. Language, work, art and cosmology are confrontations with materiality and as materials in themselves. Constants humiliate the person, they point to a foolishness of opposition. They deny the person's time, they make his time as nothing, they stand for time over the person. The person's constant is his struggle with materiality; the matter of material and the matters of his relationships to it. The person views his time out of and into constants. He makes language his own and coins his own terms. His struggle with material is against its infinity and against his own finitude. Constants are the person's bond with the lumpen reality, with his objects, inhuman objects and the world of objects. The potential is to transcend constants, to constantly change them, to make a permanent change, to create a wholly new object that marks the person's time on the timeless face itself. The potential is to transcend constants into new forms and expression of constants that will outlive the living memory of the person.

Contradictions emphasize social relations, other persons; people at large. Contradictions penetrate space and time — social space and social time — by poetic or mystical patterning. The realities are the properties of the person. As far as he can tell his eye can see that his life, for example, is solitary and shared. The metaphors for contradictions are yet more contradictions: endless paradoxes of understanding to express understanding. The problem is being lost in contradictions, of being tossed back and forth. Being nowhere with no one all the time and none of the time. Contradictions contain the person: confine him with opposing alternatives repugnant in exclusion. Contradictions hurt the person; trap him always from all sides. Contradictions make for the rightfulness of a proper place in life and the impossibility of arriving and staying there.

The person houses his contradictions impressing them upon

17 A theory of the person

himself and, expressing them to other persons. The person's struggle with contradictions is in itself a contradiction; he does not want what he knows he must have. The energy generated by contradictions is the most useful and useless. The person makes innumerable moves and each time arrives at a position where he must make one more. The problems are those of making time and marking time; clearing a space only to vacate it. Contradictions make sense and nonsense of the person's economics. How is the person to use his resources? How is he to spend his time? How can he ever not be wasting time? How is it that he is marking time and suspended in it? How can he use what is always using him? Is there any future which is not an aimless recreation of the present? Is there any future with others?

Making time and making friends are the two simplest representations of the consequences of contradictions. Because there is social time — there is the personal time of events; of times spent to do something eventful. Because there are times of sociability — there is the personal event of solitude — doing nothing, stopping time in its tracks by having all the time in the world. The potential of contradictions is just this fluency, of movement between opposites and the movement making an opposite real. The potential is of discarding clocks and feeling every second, of emptying isolation and running to company. The potential of contradictions is contradictory of being almost dead and nearly alive; the potential lies in the realization of contradictions and of changing.

The person's perspectives, I have said, are problems and potentials. He is equipped to relate to them and use them. They take him to nature, to matter and to space and time. They cover his world in a recognizable way and in a way in which he can recognize what he is doing and thinking about. Constants, necessities and contradictions *emphasize* contexts. They do not specially own them or exclusively refer to them. It is the person who relates to his contexts. His compartmentalizing into contexts is not exact. Rather it is necessarily inexact. For the person is whole and his contexts are fractured. To the person contexts are imprecisely separated; while to himself they are seen as his world. The person's vision is unitary: that which he sees is variously paralleled by the expressions of constants, necessities and contradictions.

The person sees all that there is to be seen; nothing old or new is missed. The person puts all together; takes all of all perspectives; makes all of all there is. All perspectives are necessary to him and for him; none are sufficient. The person is constructed by his own construction of perspectives. The perfection of the construction of the person is in his full reconstruction of reality. The perfection of the person is in the complementarity of the three perspectives in him and for him. The theory of the person is thus a trialectical theory.

A trialectical theory

Wishing to express my reasoning in an orthodox manner I have come to believe in the possibility of trialectical relationships. Perhaps I mean no more than thinking in threes or being able to hold three things in one's head at the same time. But perhaps it is possible that three parts of man are dialectically related and that one such part is a dialectic in itself. Thus I feel bound to coin the neulogism 'trialectics' and proceed to its usage.[6]

To live in the present is to be prey to distraction.
To live in the past is to force memory to provide meaning.
To live in the future is to negate responsibility.

For me a redundancy has entered dialectical thought. I am

19 A theory of the person

thinking of its closedness, its potential for reification and it being primarily a didactic mode. By closedness I refer to the 'on the one hand and on the other' sing-song usage to which it has been subject and turned into a fixity of systems. By reification I mean the representation of a mechanical collision — of two 'things' fighting it out as to which is cause and what is to be effect. And by didactic mode I mean the ease with which distinctions can be made between the dissimilar only to make one single concrete 'point'.

I admit that trialectical propositions may be awkward. I advance them because they are possible — and to me fruitful — in relating the person. Further, I would suggest that trialectics are irresolvable, that the ideal makes it important to look and less important to look for 'answers'.

Each of the parts I have designated is in a dialectical relationship with the others. And this relationship is simultaneously:

        a problem
and   an energy
        a proposition of directions.

Please bear with me a little longer while I gradually make the argument more specific.

The three perspectives on and of the person encompass problems, potentials and 'thrusts'. The person lacks nothing nor lacks for nothing. And each perspective relates to the other. *Each perspective is in a dialectical relationship with another making the third perspective a dialectical ground for this figure.*

Three sets of such positions hold:

Contradictions contradict constants in the contradicting context of necessities.

Contradictions contradict necessities in the contradicting context of constants.

Constants contradict necessities in the contradicting context of contradictions.

20 A theory of the person

Taking three facets of each perspective we can exemplify the propositions.

Table 1 shows the three facets.

Table 1 The three facets

Contradiction	residence *vs* travel
Constant	work
Necessity	ageing

The propositions then reads as in Table 2.

Table 2 The propositions

Residence *vs* Travel	*vs*	work	whilst ageing
Residence *vs* Travel	*vs*	ageing	whilst working
Working	*vs*	ageing	whilst residing *vs* travelling

Each feature can be taken in turn and all should be taken to reveal the dilemmas, drive and directions of the person. Dilemmas are produced by the trialectics of problems and directions are produced by the trialectics of potentials. Drive — if this be possible — is the trialectic 'itself'.

In making these propositions 'trialectics' may have become clearer. Simply put, trialectics maintains that no contradiction operates in a vacuum and that the setting of the dialectic is in a dialectical relationship to it. The product of a trialectic is a point of arrival, a position of extreme conflict and a point of departure. As expressed before there is a contradiction between two perspectives, one of which is a contradiction and both of which contradict a further perspective.

The perspectives are united, then, by the trialectical relationships between their features. Moreover, each constant, contradiction and necessity can be elucidated and ramified until it contains 'all' of that perspective. For example, an account of work can be made to account for its creative aspects (art), its technical terms (language) and its plateau of vision (cosmology). It is not helpful to do this but it does illuminate the coalescent nature of facets of a perspective and does simplify the complementary nature of trialectics. Such simplification approaches more directly, too, the sorts of answers so often sought. For example why is there so much movement and change in the person? Why does the person celebrate being the same person who has changed? Why is there so much habit and seeking of novelty?

Trialectical relationships are a struggle and successful; in this sense they are favourable. There is a beneficial complementarity between constants, contradictions and necessities.

There are three alternative diagrammatic representations of the trialectic: the person. Two draw upon popular graphics in the social sciences and make reference to problems that the theory may contain. A further diagram is drawn to make a change.

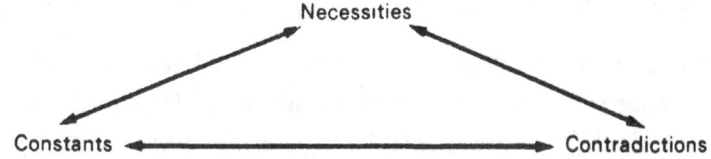

Figure 1 The trialectics of the person as interactions

Figure 1 emphasizes the interrelationship of the perspectives and offers no necessary form. The figure conveys mutual influence and movement. It is as if messages are continuously travelling around the person conveying information from one perspective to another and changing its view. Implicitly, however, there is a suspicion that the big business is at the top. The apex is a position of marginally greater importance. This figure can be redrawn twice again putting constants then contradictions at the top to make the equivalence of perspectives clear.

Interaction diagrams give rise to problems of mutual influence; as to exactly how trialectics are felt and as to how an interaction may be simplified to reciprocal causes and effects. Their weakness in this case is to make the tension of trialectics less important than its paths.

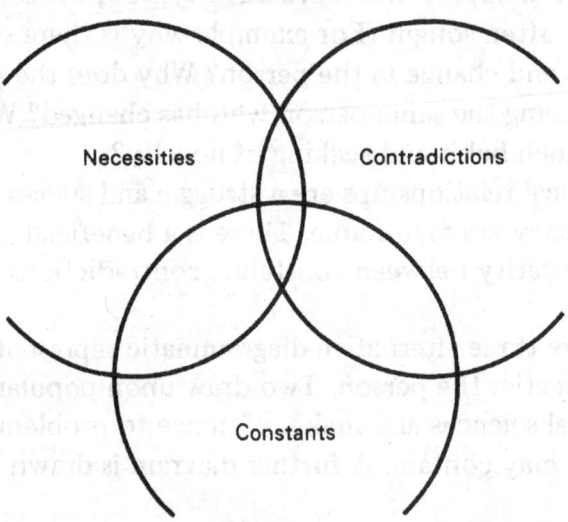

Figure 2   The trialectics of the person overlapping spheres

Figure 2 emphasizes the distinctiveness of the perspectives, their interpenetration and yet boundedness. This pattern gives equality to the perspectives by taking them clearly into each other. It seeks the problem of boundaries; of how each perspective remains distinct and how the perspectives flow

23 A theory of the person

to and from their contexts. The boundary of the person becomes the biggest problem. How the person stays together and does not collapse into contexts becomes the problem. The weakness of this figure is that it so firmly locates the person in milieu that he needs rescuing from it.

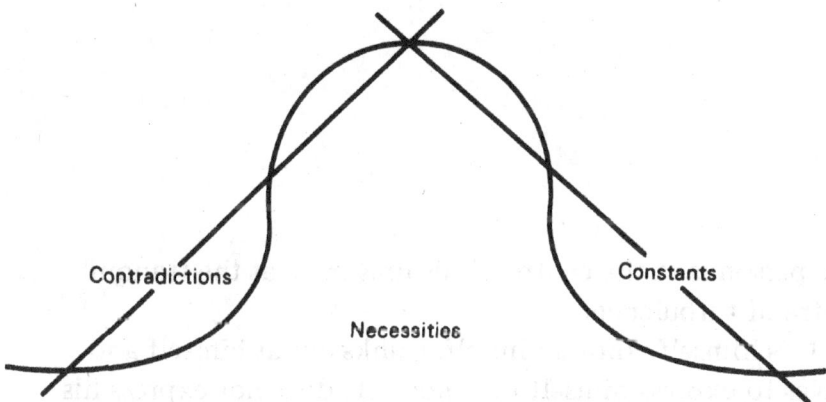

Figure 3 The trialectics of the person as a metaphysical sign

Figure 3 is a more pictorial representation. It creates an image of the being. The rhythm of elaboration and reduction that are necessities surge upwards and downwards from beginning to end nearly completing a circle. Constants and contradictions overlay this shape strong, unbending crossing each other once and necessities twice at top and bottom. Figure 3 emphasizes perfection. It refers to Alpha and Omega: beginning and end. The problem with this diagram is that it leaves little to say!

⑤

I hope the picture is clear, but even if it is not, what follows may be of interest. For when a person believes in being a person he may be trusted at first and disbelieved fruitfully at the end.

3

The cup of constants

The person is at the centre of his universe;[1] at the tranquil centre of turbulence.

He is himself, knows himself, thinks about himself and strives to express himself to others. He does not express his 'self'. He puts himself into what he says and does. His ideas, like himself, are incommunicable and impenetrable. His words stretch inadequately to cover his imagery and barely succeed in pointing to the direction of his thought.

The person is inarticulate for his own purposes. Admire as he may the expression of others he cannot make their speech his own. The more he strains to possess it the less he grasps.

His words are his own. He has taken from a living language, from its users and literature, a vocabulary. His vocabulary does not contain fixed meaning. Its more resilient components are personal clichés — phrases, borrowed or made — that express a matter of opinion as a matter of fact. Personal clichés are so filled with experience, with repeated application, that their communicated quality is of finality.

The person invests all of himself when using words. The struggle is dismal, desultory and destructive. The person despairs of words. His language is inadequate for his pictured thought and a poor substitute for action. Words beget deeds. The person is more impressed by what is done than by what is said. When told of bold plans in which he is not a part the person waits to see.

25 The cup of constants

The person can always acquire new words. In contrast to the ideas and actions they suggest; they are but a hint of what is real to the person. His thoughts are real, his actions are real and the outcome of thoughtful action is real. The person's achievements are symbol-objects. They are concrete representations of himself. In the finished object he can see his flusters and fluency of thought. Each mistake is a turning point where development was redirected and the error overcome.

The person thinks about what he has done and what he could do. Putting these thoughts into words ends them. The person puts his feelings about action into words and in this feeling there is a clear evaluation. These feelings are the small, daily benchmarks of biography.

Language becomes rigorous as it expresses what is valued and what is to be done. It cannot become rigorous *in vacuo*. The person has language; has his own vocabulary: and is happier with the thoughts and deeds which his words serve.

The person thinks of matter and meaning. By matter he means what he needs to live. He thinks of earth, water, air and fire; of eating, drinking, breathing and the shelter which is warmth. These biological needs form the habits of his being. His habits entail the production of what he needs and the preservation of what he continues to need. The person makes; wears, breaks and mends. He is his crucial resource in the production and reproduction of the resources he consumes.

The person's production habits constitute work; work being the person's staple physical, practical and thoughtful process.[2] Work is about replenishing the earth and taking from it. Replenishing abundance increases abundance. Work does not provide direct meaning for the person — it is a meaning of a particular nature. Its meaning is the what, where, when and how of his production, consumption and care for the qualities of his life-sustaining processes. Physical work, for example, has its particular meanings. It belittles the body which then sings with exhilerated exhaustion. It is accursed in that mistakes must be fully made good. It is an immediate struggle and in saying 'it will have to come' there is the sharp sense of an eternal struggle.

In work, then, the person makes a meaning. It is his reflections on this process (his care for qualities) that constitute the bones of his cosmology — what might be called his proper meaning. The person does not have an integrated set of attitudes, beliefs or faith. He has a vision. His vision is his way of seeing things; his ordering of the relevance of subjects and objects. People; animals; places; sights and startling memories populate his thought. He wonders about them; their properties, differences and bearing on himself. The person's thoughts on others are the most startling. Their motives are of endless interest; their faces clear with a moment's memory and their current feelings a constant unknown. An endless curiosity is engendered by the question 'where are they now?' A presumptive sadness accompanies the question 'who are they now?' Why do people change? Why do friends fail to find each other? Why do families quarrel?

The question 'why' carries the person into his cosmos. His questions are unanswerable yet he can be fascinated by interminable descriptions. His fascination can be firm if he can stop asking questions and listen to the sound answers of unity.

All cosmologies transport the person to a plane from which questions are foolish. 'The world is like it is because it is the world' say cosmologies helpfully. The person can marvel at differences rather than be disturbed by them.

The person's cosmology can be religious or secular. In either context the person shapes up to time and can shape his art. The religious cosmology protects the future of mortals from mortals. The secular cosmology projects the future of men by men. In both unity will come as the seeds of synthesis exist now. Men's souls can be saved; society can be sensible, sensitive and just. Cosmology is about the natural world —

In matters of action the person is scientific — scientific in the capacity to construct an experiment and sceptically relate initial theory to on-going practice.[3] Science is a personal act. 'The theory of . . .' indicates an idea put into practice that works. It works because it suggested what was to be made and how it was to be done. In microscopic terms what was to be made was a product whilst macroscopically the achievement is the beginning of a process in which new achievements can be made.

The person theorizes on that which can be seen and reached. The person talks of that which can be coming into being. His theory is one jump ahead of current practice and he devotes his practice to produce that which becomes obviously true. The person is a theoretician *and* the first practitioner. His science takes his resources and courage in private speculation. His theory is practical though socially it remains 'a theory' until others find that its cryptic, skeleton, question fleshes out into a beginning and a direction.

The person as scientist makes and remakes ideas, shapes novel products and novel forms of product appreciation. He loosely unifies his language, work, art and cosmology even if apparently solely engaged in one of these 'spheres'. The person's actions are scientific: reasoning what to do next and its relationship to what happens next. The person's science is traumatic for the person. But this duress can be dramatized unnecessarily. Traumas are more properly trials of reaction rather than action.

The person learns his reactions by reaction; a trauma is the trial of this adjustment. A trauma is an immersion in the past or future which terrorizes the present. Times of experience are ripped out of their sockets.[4]

During the first time of a task the person is frightened of making mistakes. Afterwards the mistakes are the most evident facet of the task's products. Their correction is the basis of the second attempt at the same task. On the third occasion the person is guessing the mysteries and formulae of

27 The cup of constants

as far as the eye can see — answering questions about the ordering of this nature.

The person's art has a place in his cosmology. It is an act of respect, love, worship and awe. The immediate *does* matter; now is significant; in fact it is all important. The person's art pleads with others and pleases others. 'Come on over and see how good it feels' is a call to action and a promise of peace.

Whereas work for life-support is somewhat repetitive art for life-worship is inclined to be revolutionary. Work habits are comforting — the person develops a knowledge of materials and their handling. Art activity is a different therapy. Each new expression is dissonant with the 'old person', it is an hard-edged comment on the person made by the person. Art objects are impractical in the sense of reminding the person of the old — of the trail of debris behind him.

Each object is a definite statement of the person — making revolution by rounding off the past and marking no limits on what he does next; where what he does next holds most of his attention. Art to the person is to some purpose. The purpose is 'not a mirror but a hammer for shaping reality'.

Work and art are not separate actions either in mind or in action. Work and art pass time. They expend time by involvement in the various actions. They measure time by their products. 'What I have done' is a mechanism in the person's autobiography and his contribution to the biography of the place where his action was made. Work and art have a further meeting in music-making: when the play side of work and the subject side of art produce a total transcient effect. In practice, too, beauty and utility are co-existent and inseparable. Some actions exhibit this unity more clearly than others. The person decorates himself in clothing; cosmetics are care over the fractions of body still evident. The person's choice of clothes is a creative act and thus his immediate symbolization of himself.

29 The cup of constants

the process. He seeks laws and recipes that are operational and sequential; that give guides for detection and correction of falsehoods; formulae that are stepping-stones through a mystery. The better placed the stones the more the path is illuminated. Tasks in triplication are the preamble to skill; the forerunner of mastery. This learning is common to action and reaction: to the person as scientist and serialist. In action the person is especially learning the form of doing. In reaction the person is learning the content of feeling. Consequently the person as scientist is an experimentalist and as serialist is an experientialist. The account of learning by reaction needs an account of 'virtues' brought as skills to the sustained shock of suffering.

A trauma, an external action that denies the present by direct threat and suspension in known past and unknown future, is recognized by the person as a mistake. The mistake is regarded with humility. Diligence is applied with perseverance; upheld and contained by intelligence, confidence grows to correct the recognition and reapply the person to the redefinition of the trauma. The trauma is no longer his, but is a necessary mistake. Whilst the external action is both 'inside' the person as a mistake and 'outside' the person as a threat, adjustment can be made and seen. A trauma is a death and rebirth, a baptism of fire; the necessity of ashes before the phoenix.

In contrast with creativity, however, both action and reaction are small-scale transcient perspectives on the person's learning. For creativity does not spring from wanting to do something or having to do something. Creativity is more than a synthetic union of action and reaction. It is the conduct of experiential experiment. The person makes himself unknown, to change how he knows himself. Creativity is a conscious striving for the impossible: a new good life that determines all action and reaction as wholly beneficial. The person musters the moment and muddle of his cosmology for a great leap and lands a fraction further. Creativity is not the vital spark in particular works of genius. It is a shorthand for the person's capability to telescope life; to live a number of lives with intensity and an essential property in the living of his life. It is the mode of learning that enables the person to say 'I' and imbue his meaning with validated individuality. The person is creative to the point of being sure of himself whilst surrounded by mirrors and masks. As with action and reaction the person has to learn what to do next, what to do under strain and how to recast himself. He needs to learn from these acts.

Though the content of the person's creativity evades general specification a form for the process can be suggested. Creativity has the form of a cycle with six poetically titled phrases. No attempt will be made to anchor these stages in what might be created. As has been argued, what is really being created is the person by the person.

First there is the leaving. Leaving is a burst into estrangement. Seeing oneself, observing oneself. Smiles and sombreness of recognition. The realization of how long things have been so. Leaving averts the person's eyes from the past without directing them to the future. The person looks around him; gradually differentiating making from what is made; disentangling law from custom; need from habit; love from loyalty. Leaving neither gets the person anywhere nor takes him anywhere. Leaving is momentous and yet a marginal relocation. From this new position of subtlety the person looks around.

As understanding becomes more direct the person enters the flowering. The leaving turned a corner: structured an epoch. The flowering is the blossom of new shoots; an epoch in being. The person shoulders sensitivity; sharpens wits; brings tired senses to a novel openess. Opening out, and yet unable to move, the person experiments with unaccustomed passions and actions. In flowering, the strain of leaving is realised. The person simply notes what is changing. The person has the fullness of a scholar. All is interesting. Nothing

31 The cup of constants

is unimportant. Form, pattern and logic hold fascination: for the person is outside them, fulfilling new forms of leaving.

Flowering intensifies to travelling. Giddy transportation across lush and avid textures. Sensitivity crowds to command movement. In a relentless, effortless drive to distil what he has learned the person quits the leaving entirely. The person's mind, interest and aspiration roam without rest. Settling on nothing with no need for roots adjacent to any inhabited place. The person makes his own way, as if directly, to a new place. A place without rancour, a place peculiar in that no person has found it before. A place from which to start; in which the burgeoning energy can be directed afresh. The person has travelled to a place where his roots can roam.

As the travelling centres the person develops the deepening. There are ramifications to his new place. There are skills of analysis and expression to be learned. Clearly in deepening the person propounds a vocabulary: his words to describe his voyage and to account for his finding. In deepening the person is a seeker of certainty. He can hold his place but he cannot secure it. The tremulousness of leaving; the kindness of flowering; the breathlessness of travelling compound in the new effort: to know where he is and not where he has come from. The deepening; the construction of broad easy pathways is a categorical spoilation of effort and achievement. The person rests and in so doing enters the saddening.

The saddening is the person's shifting of purpose — unease at the imperfect landscaping of his find, disease of the wantonness of expression. Words are failing; work becoming generally repetitive; art becoming a cynical cipher and cosmology crumbling under the weight of interminable justification. The person tarries wanting to leave; waiting to leave. Saturated with sadness the person hobbles creativity with qualifications or leaves again. The person leaves when he remarks on the slight distance he travelled in contrast to the efforts of the deepening.

Creativity, then, is the learning of personal time; the

person's constructions of his own epochs and the relevance to the person of the epochs he has made. In crude terms, the person can do something creative if he can recreate himself. Creativity offers no simple scheme. Action is scientific and reaction is traumatic it has been said. Creativity is not as easily labelled; it is a process through which the person moves as he moves and finds himself. Creativity is the person's wholly personal experiment and struggle with stress. Creativity is a cycle in which the person moves mountains and inches. For essentially if action is staggering forward and reaction staggering backwards creativity is the person on his beam end.

In learning action, reaction and creativity and simultaneously learning from them the person has reflection. 'Hindsight is 20/20'.[5] The person remembers each new content of knowledge and notes its contrast with what is known. Reflection is a fuller process than retrieval however. Reflection is a process of demystifying the past. A remembering is an interpretation: the person observing himself as an actor and discerning the circumstances of the performance's production. The person sees the context of his action, what others did to him, and appreciates the criteria that make his actions now seem reactions. The adaptive mechanisms: the secrecy, sycophancy and sabotage he used. The person thus sees the current relevance of such mechanisms — that they are the lies of the past. Such mechanisms still being enacted are living a lie. Their usage is overcome by the person. The devices of reaction thus divorced from the demands of action are consigned to the past: still to be known, always to be remembered, never to be used. The past demystified in this way, is behind the person. Demystification is the ground clearance for the person's facing to the future. Reflection is recall and revision to some purpose. Reflection brings fullness, though not finality, to the learning in action, reaction and creativity. In no especially systematic way, the person continuously takes stock and revokes the significance of that which has gone.[6]

33 The cup of constants

Learning is neither arduous nor repetitive. The person's effort is in the repeated applications of what he has learned. Learning genuinely never stops. Learning is perpetual; realization and response; awareness and consciousness; enlightenment and liberation. Action, reaction, creativity and reflection compound as the person's equipment for acquiring possessions and possessing himself.

But it is love that bonds the person's constants: that seals his celebration.[7]

Love is the person's joy with that which he is not. Love is the negation of self — the ultimate presence of the other. Love is *between* people and *for* things. Love is attachment and adhesion. Love is the struggle for selflessness which necessitates the egocentricity of the person. Love is an expression; a giving out of the obvious as a token of the sublime. Love is a projection. A throwing out of self; out beyond the reach of the person; and so is irretrievable. The person does not want his love back. The person does not want to be loved, he wants to love: to be able to love another is to be able to be loved. Enabling another to love by love is being in love.

This love of the person is full; without conceit or calculation. Love as sexuality, as attraction, as infatuation, as excitement is an affair perpetuated by love. Love is an event; a singularity; the end of experience; the dawn of peace.

Love as an affair is impotent; nothing is produced but love and that was there in full measure from the beginning. Love as an event is potential for love, is being felt and given, is said and made. Love is sexuality to be sure, but only in the sense of 'all of life's a dream and dreams are only part of dreaming'. The sexuality of love is something clearly different, ego can be destroyed as well as dissolved, the person can collide as if in nuclear fission as well as coalesce as if a deliquescent salt. Love can rise up as thunder and storm the earth. Love is created by the person and can destroy him. Only love can destroy the person before death; all other feelings empty him whilst love is a constantly pressing surfeit, an ensuing suffocation, a submergence in a pool of tears.

Love is obviously at the heart of communication. Love always anticipates understanding; makes sympathy straightforward; rejects empathy as an empty hope for spirit possession; draws on listening as a strength; speaks only as a feeling honestly felt and as advice thoroughly given. Communication begins as the person talking to a person. It continues as talking with one another. The translation was possible through trust; with pleasure in being together; with being arrested by the thoughts of the other, with a breathlessness in wording what is told to one another. Of necessity the persons are close; of necessity, too, they must touch and appreciate each other's warmth and texture without distress or disturbance. The electricity that the communication is generating is earthed in the other as an increasingly respected generator. The communication is making power in each person and they are freely using it with each other.

There is no upset at differences either. In fact differences are 'of the essence', the persons are telling each other about each other and rejoicing in what they can say that is fresh to another. And what they are told contrasts with their own understanding and yet appears to offer insights on it. The persons appeal to each other; they have time for each other; other interests are suspended; all interests are amenable to examination, external pressures are relaxed and internal pressures mount. But neither person bursts: they emerge; spring forth; give out in words like a song. They can definitely say what they definitely feel. In 'talking with' there are the signs of 'moving towards', of approaching the other clearly; of touching without fear and — with this realization — the pleasure of getting closer in the simple knowledge of ever enlarging difference and effort to express the marvel of being together and 'light years apart'.

Love is being felt — sexuality stirs; the persons are

35 The cup of constants

possessing each other without appropriate actions. They pass through a phase of admiration — of frank expression, of attraction of guiding their gaze to the many parts of the close other especially to the parts of the face now speaking in harness with words.

The persons are 'making together'. They are making gestures and phrases fully their own, they are reaching new realizations easily. As each expresses himself vital observations are made on this self which are attributed to the perspicacity and readiness of the other self. The conversation, the expressions, are creative. The persons create for each other as a response to each other's creative suggestions. In making together anything is said. The content of communication is boundless. The communicators bound together anywhere at each other's suggestion. Speed is being made together; abstraction is an observation tower on each other's travels.

This making together produces new forms of awareness and especially shared phrases; ideas model to words, together fashioned, and exactly say what was being talked about. The persons have produced an idea and a means of referring to it. Each frequently refers back to this idea and grants it status. The idea is now being used and the persons are 'talking about'. They are talking about anything as if filling in the map so sparsely charted. They are running down: the play after work. Relaxing the intensity, finding fun, and annotating their find. As 'talking about' rests further into appreciable silences the persons are 'withdrawing to them'. Returning within themselves refreshed and weary to continue the dialogue: taking a memory of the other person to a levelling: a reconciliation with other momentous events: the part of the idea communicated in panoply of ideas; an attempt to see just how much change has been created; how much more freedom made. These problems are also topics, the memory of face; words; ideas; the relevance of the idea in the person's picture and living of life. They are the ground topics of the next 'talking to' and facilitate faith in its painless procession to 'talking with'.

36 The cup of constants

Communication takes love and makes love, seeks and finds sexuality; shimmers with feeling; laces thought with giving and taking. Communication as exchange leaves no trace but debt. Communication as love leaves all traces of a person touched; leaping and laughing together and, vitally, leaving each other more than each other. No dismissal; no dismal loss of face or faith. Communication produces the person; communication promotes the person, a person who can be interesting, understood, played with delightfully — a person who can be loved, is being loved and is loving.

This is not to say that communication is sexual in intent; it is rather to suggest that between persons there is an awareness of the homosexual or heterosexual situations which they conjointly constitute. And sexuality for the person has one further relevance which makes its relevance as an identity and as relational necessity sensible. Sexuality is inseparable from the orgasm. It is not possible to love without leaving self and it is not possible to find self in love without knowing this love unutterably lost in the making of mutual ecstacy.

The orgasm is the liberation of the person by interpersonal means. It is the making of something by two someones. It is the rending as under of every cherished connection. It is a matter of freely enabled single concentration. An orgasm in the person is an awareness of an orgasm in the other person. An orgasm makes the persons what they are not, disconnected, drawn doubly in dissolution having disappeared into each other for a second. And in that same second having synthesized mind and body in one urgent, vital effort.

The orgasm stills the disquieted heart; brings peace of an impossible kind; a peace of the person, a momentary completeness in an incomplete being with an incomplete life. The orgasm is death and rebirth of the person with the collusion of another person. The orgasm is the living end of sexuality, a burst of feeling bigger than fear and smaller than hope.[8]

37 The cup of constants

The person transports himself into herself and back again at the moment of climax and cannot remember a thing. Simple pleasure, a finite absolute joy, an impossible victory over the possible.

The awareness of what the orgasm means carries the person further into its personal significance. The simplicity of its proof for the other person; the seal it sets; the making and keeping of a promise simultaneously rendered; a bond; the possibility of its outcome; the reproduction of another person, part peopled by both persons. For the energy, if it be such, is not sexual energy but an energy of relational necessity.

☯

In conclusion

Certain separations have been made to explicate some person processes. Separations were made between matter and meaning, work and art, domestic knowledge and cosmology; language being given as an entity. Such separations are fallacious if applied to the person as categories or as compartments. They are too clean, reasoned and adamant. Their co-existence is general to and in the person. It is not that the person is confused. It is rather that the analyst is thinking about work whilst the person is doing his thinking about his work. He owns and uses his properties. The person is within his cosmology, for example, as he pours his cosmology into his action.

Language, work, art and cosmology, creativity, love, communication and orgasm are commonplace universals in thinking about the person. They are the accepted facets of personal culture.

4

The plain of contradictions

Contradictions are themes to experience. They pervade the person's life by way of his awareness of opposites, his movements between them and the temporary nature of any settlement he makes. Can it be that within the person there is a nomad and a settler: a light-loaded steppan wolf and a companionable grower of food and maker of comfort? Does having a home make it possible to travel freely and does travelling freely depend on having a home to go to? Both activities are intrinsic to the person. In travelling he takes in the lives of others, in nesting he gives out his own distillation of life. Travel broadens experience and residence establishes it; branches and roots, flight and firmament. Home is the place where the person really considers his work and art to be. Home is having a place, a personal space, room to exist. Home becomes a confine, a glass prison, if the person cannot leave it. The person is rootless, a wanderer, a perpetual immigrant without a home. The person is attracted and aversed to his home, to leaving it, to being away, to staying away and to returning. To having everything and having nothing.

The person relates to his property in a complementary contradiction. The person is a miser and philanthropist. He hoards daily; he knows his possessions however few or numerous. He gives away regularly; he fails to retrieve losses

39 The plain of contradictions

often. He cannot have all he wants and does not want all he has. The person is beset with how to acquire more objects and how to divest himself of yet more objects. His home is a warehouse of imports, treasured possessions and potential exports. His classifications remain the same as he continuously reclassifies his property. Possessing nothing is impossible. Only birth and death are naked. Possession of everything is the person's nightmare; to drown in a sea of his own making. The person is niggardly and magnanimous. Without effort he acquires and divests himself. Towards lumpen material the person is careful and careless. He can take it or leave it.

Sexuality is a further contradiction. Sex is a property of relationships, and a possession in those related. Sexuality may be simplistically the outgoing force as ageing is an incoming force. So discussed a topic is sex that it is not possible for the author to assume any common understanding in the term's usage. No other meaning will be given to sexuality than a personal problem, potential and promise; a perpetually pleasing worry.

As this enquiry is on the person then, the problems can conveniently be expressed in the first person:

Am I man or woman?
How should I be as man or woman?
How should I be towards men and women?

The first two questions turn round on each other. If I am a man then this is how I should be. If I should be as a man then that is what I am. However, the category is about a content: the category man is about what a man is and how these properties are expressed in relationships.

The person is located somewhere in the duality of sexes with a dual significance. This means that the person is, or is not, either, or both, of two sexes. And it means crucially that the two sexes are opposite. That any account of the person's position is his placing in a world of two definite poles. Men and women can think the same things; like the same things and make the same things. That which they are is opposite.

40   The plain of contradictions

As opposites they complement. As similars they would supplement. As opposites constant conflict is understandable. As opposites constant harmony is understandable. As opposites there is lifelong fruitful fascination with one's opposite. Men and women contradict each other. The person thus is either man or woman and enjoying the contradiction of the other or lost in some *ad hoc* combination and each finds the conflicts and complements of those the same as itself. What then are masculine and feminine that makes them such good opposites and bad composites?

The masculine is active and recreative, the feminine is passive and procreative. The masculine is outgoing and symbolic, the feminine is receptive and real. The masculine is of dreams and visions, of things to be made, of wonders to be realized. The feminine is of intoxication, of things that are born, of beauties realized. The masculine struggles without whilst the feminine holds within. The masculine shouts and the feminine cries. The masculine is independent and the feminine dependent. The masculine is weak, seeking, searching, suggesting and destroying. The feminine is strong, finding, accepting and preserving. The masculine reaches for the sky, the feminine works with the earth.

Volumes of pious, beautiful poetry have been written on masculine and feminine principles by Eastern mystics. For this duality does seem both pervasive and fundamentally productive. The hard phallus and warm womb are so opposite that something must come of their co-operation — as something must come from their conflict. The point is quite simple for the person at seed, masculine and feminine are poles apart and in direct contrast with each other. For example the feminine reproduces, procreates new beings. The importance of this process must be its outcome of the new being that begins. The masculine produces, recreates new things; the importance of this process must be the process itself; each act makes for more newness more involvement in an unknown, unsecured product. When dealing with the same

41 The plain of contradictions

act the masculine holds the process sacred and the product profane and the feminine the reverse. They can but admire the other's concern, confidences, capabilities and competences.

The person makes a choice between principles. The person being masculine and feminine is forced choice, a false choice and a fearful choice to sustain. Both principles are at work in the person. But as with other contradictions the more deliberate the choice the more liberating its polar opposite seems. Contradictions are not to be resolved but to be sustained. For even though each can be elevated to the status of big daddy dialectic, this elevation simply subordinates other dialectics. Cosmologies arbitrate between dialectics in the sense of judge one as one to be at the base of cosmic forces. The most I can do here is list dialectics that I know to be true. Out of choice I would make that of solitude and sociability equal to that of place, possessions and sexuality.

The person is born of a mother, lives alone and dies alone. The person is a physiological fact. Within a body; between ears; behind eyes standing on two feet the person is locked up within himself. That which bolts the person down with finality is the physical structure of his being. Within this domain the person has himself. Because of this fixity of physical territory there is a necessary problem of being alone and of being alone with or without other persons.

It is facile to represent aloneness or company as the person's big problem. The person may wish to be alone or may wish to break his fast by sharing with other persons.[1] These wishes are, however, produced by circumstance. For as there is a problem in aloneness and company so there is a promise of the fruits of solitude and sociability. It is easier to represent both conditions as pitiful and pitiable for this heightens the awareness of the experiences and underscores the strength of the person's interests in them. Contradictions may be tragic or euphoric.

Aloneness, then, can be especially illuminated when

considered as loneliness. The body is then the territory of the person as if a mind in a body. The mind is an engine and the body a vehicle. The mind is trapped in its attendant muscular machinery. The person can observe self but not leave self. Escapism and nihilism represent an attitude of struggle with this imprisonment. The person may phantasize on breaking his chains and be overjoyed at the dramatization of this dilemma. Harry Houdini was a man bursting from appalling prisons only to return to more difficult imprisonment. His supreme effort was to transubstantiate; to escape from the prison of his birth. Nihilism is another alternative suppression of the problem. The servants of alcohol; the addicts of innumerable drugs bludgeon their mind to sleep and momentarily think themselves free.

But birth begins aloneness. The impossibility of breaking out of the body is an impossibility of breaking with the past, of separating the self of starting anew, afresh — of imprisoning fates and destinies in the body left behind.

Loneliness is, of course, much more than being unable to get out of the body either by effort of will or chemical bombardment. Loneliness is a condition of being stuck in any and every situation. The person is lonely in a crowd and lonely on his own.

In a crowd there is the terror of immediate rejection. What does the person do when told to go, or when other persons go from him? Is the rejection of one person by another an infinity of rejection? Does no one have any further use for the person? Is loneliness with others a crushing awareness of uselessness to others? Loneliness is expecially experienced in pitiful, pattern-breaking performances; in empty greetings and abrupt discharges. There is the fear of silence in company; of no one having anything to say and hardly the will to listen. There is the subtle avoidance of particular persons, of highways and cul-de-sacs made between groups well out of touch. There is the despair of gatherings and the hope of good conversation. A 'good group' for the person is two

43 The plain of contradictions

communicating as one. An achievement for the person is a group of three freely loosing themselves and their threads, learning and listening; communicating and constructing love. And so on.

This measure of aloneness and loneliness plays upon a 'time tragedy' and wrongly portrays sociability as a near impossible futility. It does, however, suggest the ways in which the problem is ever close to the person. Basically it reiterates the main point: the person is always physically alone. In this sense the person is naked; for despite all his content the person has no shell. Instead the person has a sensitive skin. Company is estranged contact, bodily sensations — crudely recognized as electricity — emanate from the person. The person vibrates, his pitch is his own; a message and a call. Reception is as sensitive as transmission particularly as the message has always one tone in its harmony 'I am alone. Who are you?' For it has been said that self is incommunicable and it is aloneness that makes it so.

Aloneness as loneliness reveals propositions despite the cost of exaggeration. Aloneness in company is particularly instructive as it depicts the vulnerability of the person in the light of the problem. Aloneness has been called a basic condition; a physical fact and this means that company is a made condition; a sought after condition, a desirable release, a real release from aloneness. Without love, and communication company sours aloneness to loneliness and makes for loneliness when alone.

The necessity of aloneness would appear to be a daily phenomenon. The person rests on his own. The rest is an unwinding, a wheeling out across interests; issues; all memories and plans. The person recasts himself and settles light upon one thing and is readily able to do one thing then another and yet another. The person feels the purposefulness of bodily position, hears slight sounds. The person alone can be willingly sad, unwittingly foolish, indecisive and small. The person alone can be aimiable, cheerful and exact. The person alone is the person deft, precise, physical actions and reactions calculably in time with purposes. The person alone can be in terror, raddled by his presence. The problems that other persons present to him ever large in his imagination. The person alone knows of discipline, real discipline, controlling himself when he could do anything or nothing until something happens. The person alone is a problem to the person unless he sees and uses its potential.[2]

The person alone can come close to an electrifying awareness of the enormity of what might happen. Prophecy, prediction, prescience and telepathy can come into appreciable strength. Yet being alone the person still cannot think everything of all things. The person alone is entirely limited to what he can do. The person alone can think as far as he is able and do little. Being alone is conducive to any activity, being together is more conducive to getting things done.

An experience I had of being alone for three weeks produced the following observations:

> You use your ears, all sounds that are not made by you are those of the world outside. You feel insufferably lonely sometimes; that your head is bursting with little worries going round and round. You know that when you meet others it is because you have chosen to seek company. You can sing, sigh and laugh on your own without excuse or explanation. You find yourself in a world with very few friends, many chance acquaintances and a lot of exasperating people. You find that some people make it their business to know where you are and how you spend your time. You are treated with a distant pity (an assumption that you find it difficult to live with yourself). And you often feel ensnared by a warm room and constant conversations. On many occasions you know you have nowhere to go and other occasions you are glad that you have one place to go and shut the door. In each

45 The plain of contradictions

conversation you unload some of the trivia of your life on the listener and you listen and watch for their inattention, offence and that change in mood which means that you, or they, will begin to leave. You rest fully and sleep like a child after a day playing with sand. You share no future with anyone; people become partners from time to time. You ache with loneliness and glory in jobs done entirely on your own — without a single word having been spoken. You know that people who do not father or mother you, boss you or police your movements, encourage you to inconvenience yourself and lose your day, are irresistible. You will soften to kindness, warm to eyes that do not pierce your pupils. You accept that one day there may be a special person — who may stay and show you other ways to live in your own home. You do not wait for a special person, you do not hope for them. You dare not hope because you have learned to cope. You cannot hope because you would flood out of yourself in devastating ecstasy. You like being alone; a pioneer in a world full of people.

These impressions represent being alone as living alone yet waiting for another. They rest on one simple idea: it's me or them. Aloneness individuates with compelling accuracy. The only unique context for the person is being alone. All other contexts are with them; with other persons. 'Them' make the person aware of the smallest differences between the persons. 'People are mirrors in whom we see ourselves' wrote Goethe. So when we are alone we cannot see ourselves and when in company we cannot see others. These quasi-deductions would be true were there simply the person and other persons. But the person achieves a productive collective reality from time to time. There is then the person, *us* and them. The ways in which the person makes this reality and the forms it takes are outlined a little later in their appropriate place. For there are still observations to be made on the properties of aloneness in me and them.

The plain of contradictions

This me and them begins at birth: the child and parents; the pupil and school; the patient and hospital. The person is individuated by parents. At the outset there is no place for the person, there are no vacancies in social networks. The person being born has no place in the lives of those that bear him. The struggle for a place is the struggle with aloneness — 'Am I me? Where are you?' The struggle can always be represented, then, as the person's struggle with his parents. Whoever controlled his development granted him more or less of a place; granted him aloneness and company; argued criteria for these states. Aloneness as a deprivation; going to your room, being banished from the hearth; getting out into the dark cold, the hellish womb of chill — nothing. Company as reward; as a rule-governed relationship, being pushed face to face but not looking, never staring and awkwardly touching the other person. Aloneness as a punishment state with no direct control apart from confine. Company as a reward-state with direct control for movement around the confine. When the person forgets his parents he confronts aloneness as a problem of choice as well as sentence, he confronts company as a problem of choice as well as withheld privilege. The person from parents has reason to fear aloneness and company: isolation and asphyxiating conformity.

Beyond parents, and the person must move beyond parents, criteria of life and death are the only ones big enough for the person's evaluation of aloneness and company. Solitude is a death of the social person; an entry by the self into the self, and end to obstruction. Sociability is the rebirth of the social person, an enterprise for the self and an end for obstruction. Only the biggest criteria will do. The person asks: 'Is this a beginning or an end to my time? Is there nothing I can do or is sharing the only thing possible now?' Solitude and sociability are burst in and out of so frequently that the shock may have numbed the person to the qualitative opposition of the states and the beneficial potential of this contradiction. It is clear to the person, however, that only if there is room

47   The plain of contradictions

in company can there be room to be alone and that only being alone produces the energy and insight to sustain company.

The fears of aloneness and company are instructive as to the problems of the properties of contexts for the person. But it should be clear that the person does not necessarily house horror in either situation. I have made a sustained effort to convey the aesthetics of necessity. Further I have made a sustained effort to reason the productives of necessity. Solitude, walking on your own; thinking without speaking; relaxing attention to easy full attentiveness to thought or material is a necessitous freedom. Sociability, getting going with them, experimenting with us; careering through thought as plan; trusting without test, achieving super-personal results with ridiculous ease is a free necessity.

Social existence is apart and together. Personal existence is in parts and altogether.

These slogans provoke some attempt at the reconciliation of personal action and social action.

Sociability, then, is an active principle to the person. The person makes, keeps and breaks his company. Aloneness is also an active principle to the person. It is their contradiction that provokes a logical relation between liberation and consciousness and it is this relation that silhouettes the person in social contexts.

The questions become — how does sociability look to the person? How does sociability give the person new sight and how does this novel vision inform the person?

The person exchanges with another person. That which controls is guilt; shame is the taking into the person the part of the other person. It is the vitality of others within the person. The person also gives himself out, he observes and jokes, he chuckles and deflates. He ridicules and teaches the other person. He shows what there is to be seen and what nonsense it makes.

In shame and humour there are no troubles of

communication. There are no gaps of understanding, no gaps of misunderstanding. The person feels the free travel in himself of others and sees the free travel of himself to others. Shame and humour socialize the person in this special way; the person is necessarily socializing himself. The person knows that he exists because he has an effect on others. He knows others exist because he has an effect on them. The person abstracts from this knowledge and appreciates the qualities of his existence with others. The person can affect his effects. He can only affect the qualities of his existence by and with these effects. As his existence is proved and his potential for qualitative effect is shown the person is alone to some social purpose.

The person unwound in this way can tolerate his lack of overall visibility; the poverty of his understanding of motive, the lack of coherence between observations. The person is giving shape and form to awareness. An impotent independence compounds that makes visible the falsity of dramatics and games. The person can hear hollowness; read between the lines; see what is going on without being told. The person is in two minds what to do.

For the presentation of self is not automatic; it presents the continuous problem of the preservation of self. Who am I? is transformed into What are they doing to me? Acting is a bluff and the precipitation of being bluff. The better the actor the bigger the problem — to be sucked in as a character and to be blown out as a caricature. Resting from the problem is being arrested by it; of settling for less than the struggle signifies, of accepting limits on personal purpose, power and progress. It is not that the person always needs to move on but that when the person resists growth he accepts belittlement.

Of course the person puts on an act and near perfects many acts. He convinces others and is a little convinced himself. What else, it is said, can he do? As a fledgeling independent he can learn; be a jack of all trades; turn to history, geography

49   The plain of contradictions

and the physical economics of fluency in crafts. He can personify innumerable objects and their intricacies; cars and guns and the workings of wheels. The person can so wrangle with contexts that his acts are endless and endlessly forming. The person can fritter his capacity for change in obsessions with constancies and comforts. The person can also recognize a corollary of his independent acquisitive interest: his agreement with good ideas is his willingness to contribute to new ideas.

The person alone to some social purpose is a rebel with curiosity. The person notes with interest the ease of exchange the engulfing simplicity of shame and humour. The person observes as he performs. In combining facility with exchange and disinterest in deception the person moves towards participation. The person has structured a trust, a good faith, a belief in people until proven wrong. The person has realized that the only investment of aloneness is in company.

The alone person so equipped for company, so aware of its false aura and true potential and action, is the stuff of leaders as well as joiners. Leaders are given weakness by the led and use the energies of the led to facilitate their mutual thoughts. The person alone is nearly sufficient with the riches of independence and almost sufficient leading dependents through poverty. The person, however, is still alone and insufficient no matter what his band of followers fulfil in his name.

The alone person is liberated from aloneness and the awareness of the meaning of aloneness not merely by leading or joining. The alone person is only liberated by sharing — by risking all of his carefully identified independence in an interdependence of a bemusingly disordered character.

And to what purpose is this contradiction amongst contradictions? How are the forces appreciated? What colours of life come from the person's contradictions? In making a guess I would answer that sadness and happiness have their energy and extremes from contradiction.

Tragedy has few synonyms which do not sentimentalize the experience. The person's confrontation with horror, obscenity, heartache and bitter inevitability make a catalogue of tragedy but only begins to indicate the anguish of his experience. The actual equation of pain and suffering is unknown and the full significance of the person's tragedy incalculable. Tragedy is hopelessness or evil which if held as a universal we might say is inevitable. The person's tragedy is especially his own. In everyday language it is an affair of the heart rather than the mind.

Tragedy is contradicted by euphoria.[3] Happiness and humour are the person's auto-destructive ephemera. Wits, intelligence and creativity make for the person enjoying himself. A joke is a revelation; an apt but askew observation; a self-observation that is fully deflating; a comment on others pungent with intimate ridicule; a commentary on things with shocking simplicity. Humour is seeing things afresh in jokes shared with others. The person jokes and laughs. As tragedy is unforgettable good humour is memorable.

In conclusion

As with the account of constants, the description of contradictions may sound like a list rather than aspects of life forces. The person's constants enlighten whilst his struggle with contradictions benight him. Yet each activates and reactivates the other. But as the account of universal constants to the person was faltering the suggestions as to universal contradiction are foolish. They necessitate such simply analogy as to cloud explicative value. Yet it is important to appreciate that the person's contradictions are battleground, army and reason to fight. They are the plains of experience to which the person goes down and is:

51 The plain of contradictions

traveller and homemaker
philanthropist and miser
masculine and feminine
alone and in company
tragic and euphoric.

The contradictions bringing his colour and scars, dreams and nightmares, dependence upon his few certain possessions and returning his shoulder to the wheel of his life-cycle.

5

The wheel of the life-cycle

The person's life cycles, it wheels across his universe, it is his companion.
 Necessities are constant, contradictory and yet have the rhythm of a continuous flow. They are necessitous as features of the person's relationship to himself. Constants and contradictions located the person in social space; in milieux or situations. The person could still be an actor with a part of complex parts. But for necessities, of necessity, the person is a thinker; an observer as well as a participant; an observer of himself whilst participating; an observer to himself. His inner voice within an inner ear. The person is an abstraction to himself; a laboratory for himself; the outcome of a continuous, rigorous analysis of his self. For necessities the person needs intelligence. With abstract thought comes intelligence; intelligence sustains abstraction; abstraction informs action and action initiates abstract thought. The person is intelligent.
 The person has a beginning, middle and end. A birth, a life and a death constitute the simplest stages in his life-cycle. Any further account of the stages takes us into the fullness of his life. Did he live until he was old or was he murdered by circumstance? Did he have a 'normal life' and proceed through all of Shakespeare's seven ages of man? Or was the process arrested and suspended to make a middle-aged prattling

53 The wheel of the life-cycle

schoolboy? Are there stages in the irresistible flow of the person's life and if so what do they mean to him? The person's life is his life-cycle. This tautology implies that the person possesses a paradox. He goes through stages that are continuous to him though they may be discontinuous in experience. The person can look backwards and forwards and see both continuity and epochs or stages. The paradox is constructed by the form and content of his learning. There is as much importance in how things are learned as there is in what is learned. For the act of learning is the process of the person learning about himself. The person learns how he is seen, the evaluations of his competence and the estimations of his potential.

The person learning something learns something about himself. Social designations of age and physical competence produce stages classified as child, youth, man and elder. It is often remarked that the translations from one stage to the next are a problem in this formulation. An existential articulation of stages argues that the achieving of one stage facilitates the leaving of its predecessor. In this view the process is accumulative rather than aggregative. A simple phrasing of an existential context is reported by Castaneda (1968, pp. 84-7) from the words of a Mexican 'bruijo' Don Juan:

> A man of knowledge is one who has followed truthfully the hardships of learning . . .
> He must challenge and defeat his four natural enemies. . . .
> Fear! A terrible enemy — treacherous, and difficult to overcome. It remains concealed at every turn of the way, prowling, waiting. And if the man, terrified in its presence, runs away, his enemy will have put an end to his quest. . . .
> He must not run away . . . And a moment will come when his first enemy retreats. The man begins to feel some of himself. His intent becomes stranger. Learning is no longer a terrifying task. . . . And thus he has encountered

his second enemy: Clarity! That clarity of mind, which is so hard to obtain, dispels fear, but also blinds . . . he must defy his clarity and use it only to see, and wait patiently and measure carefully before taking new steps, he must think above all, that his clarity is almost a mistake. . . . His ally is at his command. His wish is the rule. He sees all that is around him. But he has also come across his third enemy: Power! . . .

He has to come to realize the power he has seemingly conquered is in reality never his. He must keep himself in line at all times, handling carefully and faithfully all that he has learned. . . . He will know then when and how to use his power. And thus he will have defeated his third enemy.

The man will be, by then, at the end of his journey of learning, and almost without warning he will come upon the last of his enemies: Old age! . . .

But if the man sloughs off his tiredness, and lives his fate through, he can then be called a man of knowledge, if only for the brief moment when he succeeds in fighting off his last invincible enemy. That moment of clarity, power and knowledge is enough.

Each stage is a stage of awareness; a conquering of the preceding stage; a confrontation with the strengths and weakness of the present stage. Clarity, for example, is the transcendence of fear and the realization of impotence; of being able to get above situations without being able to get out of them or operate upon them. Clarity is soporific; knowing what is happening can become an obsession; seeing everything clearly can become a compulsion. Clarity can be narcissistic; the subtleties of what is seen can be used as a benign mirror as if complementing the sublety of the seer. Clarity can be a global enterprise and rationalize the paralysis of vision. Clarity can comfort to the extent of shielding the person's fears whilst prising open those of others. Clarity cripples action with its anticipation of utter complexity. Clarity is a false truce between fear and power — a suspension between reactions of horror and actions of terror. Clarity is being adrift or washed up beyond the tide's fetch. Clarity is the euphoric tragedy of perfecting sight and muddling deed. Clarity is an wholly hospitable confine. Fear provokes 'knees up and back into the womb'. Clarity encourages a retreat into a warm room: a den for the seer.

Each stage in an existential perspective is a stage of awareness: the grasp of an abstraction; a realization of an obvious tragi-comedy — a rest at any stage or completion through all stages produces triumphant failure.

The existential context re-produces the person's problem with, and possibility of, abstraction. Being abstract is not being different from himself, it is the general term for the processes of being himself.

The person does not pass through stages nor do stages pass through him. Don Juan's stages and turning points are thought-provoking devices. His cycle would resemble an ascending curve with four plateaux. Both stages and cycle are inflexible terms with mechanical rather than dialectical implications. So far it may have been adequate to note that the person unfolds and stages fold up; he goes out, stages flow back. The problem with a stage and a cycle is that the terms are capable of generating their own questions. For example 'what stage is the person at when . . . ?' and 'does the person's life turn full circle?' Questions more appropriate, however, are 'is the person capable of creating an endless variety of stages?' and 'is a life-cycle progressively transcendent?'

My own answer is yes to both questions. Consequently the terms stage and cycle will be used as metaphors with insecure meaning: the closest spatial representation is the shape of a double helix.[1]

Two aspects of context further shape the life-space of learning into an experiential ascent and descent. First the person gains in stature. The person acquires survival recipes: he disciplines himself in such a way as to obviate external control: asceticism is the mastery of the relation between food and hunger; the learning of breathing; listening and waiting equates self-control with control regardless of social milieau.

Part of this gain in stature is the encroachment upon mastery in determining tasks and especially their execution. As the person can only get better with repeated attempts increasing stature can be represented as apparent effortless ease — though in fact it signifies simple, singular attention to the matter in hand. The person's stature becomes ever-more adult.

The 'stature aggrandizing' process is closely related to the second contextual feature of life-space. That is the person becomes older as well as bigger. He ages. It may be felt that what has been said of learning and existential properties of stages relate age and knowledge in terms of wisdom. It cannot, however, be held that the person becomes wise. Wisdom in large measure depends upon the content of the problems that the person confronts. A life-long inquiry on the Platonic questions — What is truth? What is justice? What is right? may suffice. Whilst worrying continuously where the next penny is coming from may not. Nevertheless the person ages and there are particular perceptual features at work.

The person has more and more epochs and more ways of reflecting on them. These epochs[2] are all the more clear because ageing is the literal contraction of year and season. A year for a twenty year old is one twentieth of his life. For a forty year old a year is a fortieth of his life. Seasons come and go more quickly.

The apparently absolute contraction of time is contradicted by dilation of knowledge. The person sees fewer substances of novelty; and time and particularly a season may cloy interminably and the ageing person may be beset with boredom or the escalating struggle to discover newness.

57 The wheel of the life-cycle

Against the efforts of discovery prevails the decline of prowess. Ageing is a relentless enfeeblement. Exercise does not facilitate new feats and fitness does not obviate infertility. The person ageing takes more rest. And this decline is made obvious by the burgeoning of youth.

The person has youth and the aged on either side of him. But those that signify his ageing are the capable rather than the incapable. Youth is continuously lost by the person: ceasing to be young is more shocking than starting to be old.

The person's ageing is thus ambivalent. There are compensations in ageing — all 'ocracies' are gerontocracies. There is the cost of ageing; the person is weaker as time is speeded up and novelty harder to find. The ambivalence of ageing is also in relation to the necessity of death. The person's death is a factor in noting two general aspects to the person's problem with his life-space.

Age can become an obsession with the person. 'How old am I?' is an impenetrable imperative if made to serve the question 'Where am I up to?' Yet 'Where should I be?' can be answered in part by the person's estimation of his age. For his stage in his life-cycle and his occupancy of his life-space are his resistance to the relevance of death. Death comes at the end for the person and is coming now. The closing of his life is his completion of the cycle and the vacation of space. Awareness of the immediacy of death is contradicted by the great distance from death. Near-death occurrences strengthen the person 'Any blow which does not kill me strengthens me'. Death and life define each other. The person makes a definition along these lines for himself.

Death obviously ends an epoch. In fact it creates the person's only incontrovertible epoch. Throughout his life, however, the person is the same and different from himself. No matter how stages, eras or epochs are marked the problem for the person is his part in the life-cycle. His current position is always unclear. The person is confused in his relationship to the cycle he turns and the space he occupies. He cannot know clearly exactly where he is. The person confronts the ambiguity whether or not he seeks to resolve it by settling for repetitive certainties. He still does not know whether he is 'doing right by' his past and future. Neither can he think his way through this ambiguity; for if he tries he is ensnared by trivializing pedantry.

The first necessity related on the person has been generally titled his life-space. Yet there has been a dilemma in calling this phenomenon a cycle or a space, a destiny or a *carte-blanche*. The space has included features of action, reaction and creativity and an insistence on the relevance of ageing. A necessity in this approach is obviously more than a need or want. It is an engine and vehicle in the person's transportation, as well as his means of transpositioning of himself. The middle of his life has been accorded more importance than the beginning and the end whilst the end has been giving a reflective relevance before it occurs.

The second necessity is that of movement, of going with the flow, of seizing the time.[3]

The person alone commits the order of his independence to the anarchy of interaction. He risks his all for that is all he has. His liberation is the realization of the asset of independence: it is an investment in the potential of interdependence. Liberation then redefines exchange as an observed act and principle in such a way as to view a relationship as a productive process. What is redefined is not just exchanging to sharing; or sharing to making but also the emphasis transfers from the what is being made to the fluidity of the answer to the question who is doing the making? The answer 'we are' is the outcome of a liberation from aloneness and then a unification of consciousness.

The person and other persons do not have common interests. On meeting the person's conviction is simply the opposite. There are abysses of meaning and understanding between him and the other. Each abyss springs from their past fountains in from dissimilar language and cosmology;

59   The wheel of the life-cycle

observable through contrasting objects of work and art. The person assaults the other with his disregard for sacred topics and ritual gesture. The person appals the other with scatter-brain priorities. The person offends the other, scattering rule after rule taking more and more out of apparently infantile self-interest. The person sustains self-expression until the other has a measure of him and at this point of measurement the person rests.

Whilst resting both persons reflect on what they have said and seen. The moments of silence and outburst begin to turn. It no longer matters what provoked such incidents. What matters is the remembered tone the appeal, the anger, the calm and the complaining. The other becomes part-person in the other. More has been said than the person previously had easy words for. The person has been uneasy whilst speaking, knowing that to say more was saying things strangely. The person reflects on the crudeness of the ideas actually expressed, the apparent inability to reason, to provide reason, to reasonably permit the other person's questions. The person is curious about the other; his unfocussed curiosity focuses from time to time on the person from whom he is apart. The person remembers the other, models his reactions, notes his strengths and wonders about his inabilities. It is the memory of these powers and privations that causes the person to seek the other once more. For if chance fails to provide meeting slight calculation succeeds. The person intersects the habits of the other.

The person now informs the other of these habits; draws out of the other his economy of time. For the person fills the day with plans often before it is begun. Some part is drudgery, bought time, repetitive time, captive time regardless of feelings and conditions, some part is expansive fulfilling subtle routines; making life easier and better at a stroke. Some part is grandiose where if all goes well, with no interruption, no mistakes, a creation will fall together as if a puzzle. The problem is holding both the perfect pattern and minding every move.

The person is making claims on some room in the life of the other person. More accurately the person is making time with the other person. Less conceptually the person is asking the other to do something; to give advice; to show a skill; to settle a mind; to admire an achievement — to make love to the person by contributing to their development. The other enables the person to move one stage further. The other is an ally. The persons are qualified in each other's lives. A common present overlaps an uncommon past; regardless of what has happened the persons are fully aware of what is happening.

But the person needs to claim the other person. Each must burst into the other declaiming aloneness, wanting friendship. The question becomes why *were* we alone? The issue becomes what else can we do together? How can we guide each other? How can we affect the course of each other's lives? Can our private phantasies also be our mutual visions? Can we make something together and make something of ourselves?

As plans are expressed the friends make promises. These promises are public — the one says I will do; the other I will help. The networks of each person open and close. Past contacts are remembered and with the friend renewed. The past of each person is more fully revealed, antagonisms and ambivalences are expressed that show the stuntedness or tentativeness of previous friendships. Loose amalgams of the past and present forms occur. Each friend becomes an intermediary for the other; 'your friends are my friends'.

More and more claims are made. The friends create crises of trust. Some ideas do not materialize; some effort is withheld; some defences are constructed against such failures. Some foolish things are said; bitter memories still ache, old tragedies, relived impossibilities continuously realized. The ever enlarging friendship seems small at times. The act of co-operation has veiled the problem of time when its bond broke over the persons. Time remains a problem; my time, my ideas, my future. The friends struggle with new affection and old rebellion: with being an old rebel and a new friend.

The friends are not doing anything together. Helping each other becomes in part a chore; one is always doing what he can already do. The other is always learning what he cannot easily do and what he cannot perfect without the suspension of the other's help. The struggle between affection and rebellion intensifies but nothing seems to come of it. The friends are waiting together for others to join them and for plans that are bigger than them both.

In the enlargement of friendship has come a considerable body of terms. The terms have affected the conduct of vision and the friends viewing something together realize that something is wrong. It is not a matter of alteration and improvement; these acts are those of a change in appearance of renovation and embellishment, of alternative usage and are dispatched in a day. What is to be changed is the setting of a circumstance. Where to start is not a problem. In discussion the friends go as far back into the wrong as they can. What they wish to do is what they feel they have to do. Starting is easy, staying at it is easy. The friends are living with a common problem.

Their example is obvious. They are acting in concert; their progress reveals a plan in being. What they are actually doing is making a qualitative change in their circumstance. They are moving closer together and this closeness arouses considerable interest. For it appears that they are opposing something large solely by their own actions. They can be working separately or together; they can be discussing or designing. There is no apparent limit to the scope of the finished change and the friends are rather disinterested in achieving it now. The friends are making milestones; their shared past is symbolized; their intelligences spent on the appropriateness of the order of these milestones but not on estimations of the effort.

If the friends be male and female they will be joined by other males and females and the children of these enterprises. Other males and females ask to work and are not given jobs.

It is made clear by the friends that trust and effort are enough. For the friends have made so many symbols and changes in direction, that being together is what they desire. The general term with which we might describe more than two friends and two or more generations working in the same direction could be family. The bonds are as strong and as life-transporting as blood.

The only systematic aspects to this family is the strength of its affection within and the absence of disaffection towards alone persons. Friends meet to work and do not need meetings to corroborate effort. Each person's contribution is fully evident without measurement. The family moves together unimpressed by suggestions that they should be separate. A family is *the* family to its familiars and a movement for change in its context. The friends enlarge by birth and liberating alone persons. Each new person strengthens the family; complexifies its relationships and complements its effort. The family is engaged in social action as a corollary of its effort for qualitative change. The social action of the family is to grow into a movement. The movement grows because of what it is trying to do; each person recognizes the family effort at change as their interest, a way in which they can use their energy and as a continuous source of interest in interesting change.

The scope of the movement and the direction of its endeavours make its being and doing relevant to its context. For that which is experimental for the person is also developmental for the movement. The movement can be seen to be moving in the same, similar, different or opposite direction from its context. More relevant still, the movement is expressing the energies of a combined number of persons and representing an alternative form of expression.

It is this comparison with the direction of the social context and the occupation of social persons that makes the movement so noticeable. The movement's making of potential situations is in opposition to laboratories of social action

63 The wheel of the life-cycle

where the person's thought, word and deed are either of little consequence or not permissible for the comparative disturbance they create. In the sense that personal energies are combined the movement is political. In the sense that the movement is felt as a powerful process, the person experiences a politics. In the sense of that which is being made is at variance with that which is currently made the movement produces purposes for politics. In the sense that the movement may diverge from existing political structures the movement is one of political action.

It does not, however, take any polarization and conflict with the context for the movement to constitute the person's politics. Such occurrences may turn the movement back into families, friends and allies. It may make the movement's fulfilled purpose to affect the largest possible definition of its context. It may affect the movement by drawing fewer alone, allies and friends and encouraging births within. But the movement does not intrinsically sense boundaries; apart from realizing their existence when growth occurs. The movement is quite simply the person's politics made sensible to the person by his shared actions, efforts and ideas. The person accepts that his action is political action when he invests his aloneness in social action.

The wheels of age and movements are ever turning.[4]

6

Some thoughts which may be obvious

A note on the reasoning process

A number of concepts have been made to work hard in the theorizing. Communication, ageing and so on have been worked to offer some sense to the concern with their meaning. Each concept that has been given the treatment has been dilated with mystical properties. If you do not seek an easy answer to what is communication then you will appreciate the non-mechanical nature of the exposition. The slightest slowing down of demand for quick comprehension reveals deep and beautiful processes, processes that are sensible in their structure, subtle in their parts and sensual in their significance. The processes have been telescoped out to reveal some of these charms. In process, during processes, the person is humanizing, with natural novelty.

Thus there is an argument against dependence on false dualisms in current sociology.[1] Individual-group; individual-community and individual-society are distortions which if internalized carry disease. The person has a multitude of contexts and many constant, necessary and contradictory forms of relationships with them. Dualisms dislocate the person from situation and make the problems those of the properties of situations and how the person gets into and along with them.[2] This is not a problem for the person: it is problematic, it holds as much promise (potential) as it does trouble (problem). It may be necessary to propose dualities to teach and even perhaps to learn. But this does not make a duality true. Rather it creates one further danger of the trivializing problem of dislocation noted so far. The person is seen as incomplete in a complete context. That is, that the duality is between unequals in power and internal cohesion. The structure, the society, or what have you, has its norms and sanctions virtually complete, fully articulated encompassing all. The person has a script, costume and stage, a fragmented, fragmentary being is set to act. This duality lacks even the productive tension of better wrought dualities. There is no contradiction in this formulation. There is rather the accommodation process of a jellyfish consuming algae. However the dialectics are proposed, they are weighted for the winner beforehand. The trialectical person has a trialectical relationship with a trialectical context. The person is perfect because he holds and handles this complexity to produce his individuality. The person trialectically produces the social equivalent of his unique physical appearance. The person making completeness, is a perfect being working perfectly.

An application of the theory: normality produces abnormality: the person can be made mad.[3]

The application of a theory is a reasoning not of its parts but of the linkages holding it together. An application of atomic theory is the bombardment of an atom to release the energy linking its particles. An application of the trialectical theory of the person is the bombardment of a person to discharge the energy linking his perspectives. Enormous energy holds the person together and enormous 'losses in dialectics' are indicative of being burst apart. The normal person has all perspectives and all linkages. The mechanical person has lost one or two perspectives and has reified the remaining dialectics. The vegetable person has but one perspective and has ossified.

The normal person is healthy; perfectly perfecting himself. He has as many parts as he has thoughts; as many thoughts as there are things to think about; as many things as he can think about. Normality is a full, good life inside and out. Normality is the person's peaceful change and changes in peace.

Normal is natural to the person. Two centuries ago this observation would have seemed gratuitous. Now it is considered anachronistic. That naturalism is protrayed as reactionary is no less than a lie. It is dangerous to hold natural truths now. For natural truths rest upon a belief in abundance of people, things, food, past and future. The lie is that there is scarcity of all but people. Scarcity is an ideology. The first round of bombardment is ideological. That the world's resources are ever lower; that the earth is scorched; that people are stifling themselves and each other; that there is no room and no supplies. There *is* abundance but the person accepting scarcity accepts bargains; gifts; a whittling away of his prerogative. The argument that there is little rationalizes the provision of much less. Scarcity is produced by exploitation to further exploit the exploited. Once the person is convinced that there is not enough, not even of himself, he takes as he is taken and gives only in a calculated effort to survive. The person accepting scarcity is the person fighting for what there is, not co-operating for what there can be even more of. Scarcity lays the person low, nurtures covetousness, means that threats are of being without. Scarcity turns the person against the person. The person exploits himself; makes a bit more out of what he has in ever diminishing amounts. Scarcity weakens the content of the perspectives. Deprives them of content. Makes the person count and recount his possessions and veil them from other persons. The person who is exploited by the idea of scarcity is ripe for exploitation by other exploiters, including that of his own awareness.

67   Some thoughts which may be obvious

Exploitation makes each resource a property and structures a conflict that reduces the persons engaged even more than it expends the resource. The resource as property is valuable to the extent to which it can be withheld and expended to produce no further resources. Scarcity is the person's mercantilism making the person a merchant making nothing; taking something, using that which is taken to exploit for a slight increment in value, undermining an imagination for the resource's utility.

The exploited exploiter has a belittled stature in a diminished world. The controlling ideology of scarcity incapacitates the person to make more out of less. Exploitation is the lot of constants: words, products, art forms and faiths become properties to be held and withheld. The person accumulates for himself and the accumulation is more valuable than the content. The person is separated by scarcity from these constants and exploits to repossess them. Exploitation is the process of scarcity and property is the product of making scarce. The person is belittled by these thoughts and deeds. The first bombardment 'cuts the person down to size'. The person wants to get all he can; not get any smaller and get all he can. The person is disarmed from all but a fraction of the transformational and generational properties of constants.

The person is actively mystified and mystifying himself with the process of exploitation: the reasoning of scarcity and the result of property. He is belittled and belittling. What makes the person smaller still and bombards to a smallness of mind is an enveloping mystification of constants. Having put himself and others under control he surges to control the immutable. The person strains to control learning and ageing. Learning is restructured as conditioning: as getting something in somehow. The capacity to learn is discredited with power over the person. The person is learning to not do something; acquiring a set of operations that produce a relaxation in the directness of control. The lesson is that of obedience. By implication the reward and the reward of less control is scarce. So many things must be done to obtain them and these rewards are but a token of the full reward: for example plenty of food and self-reliance. Conditioning is the operation of scarcity on a dumb person. The person is led; hoisted when faltering; switched when erring back towards a reward: a symbol of a reward that returns him to intensive conditioning. Obedience manipulates the person and teaches acceptance of manipulation. The processes and rewards in conditioning can be modified or changed. If the person were a rat striking a bar and getting a food pellet the process might come to involve striking a person or getting a less nutritious diet. The person can become nonplussed, confused and anxious if the substance and subject of his conditioning is changing in directions of a qualitatively barren survival. But the person is conditioned into his condition. He is obedient and fearful of any greater scarcity.

Conditioning is costly. Conditioning repeats and repeats; eating into the person's time. The person's time is both what is left after conditioning and what is occupied by the conditioning repetitions. 'Doing the same thing day after day' ages the person. It takes him near a low powered automatic condition. The person is ageing and yet must race during repetitions that demand cursory attention. The person is being sapped regardless of his growth or contraction. More directly, conditioning commands a vitality, a liveliness, a youthful energy for the person to overcome its seduction to somnambulance. The person has vitality, values vitality and must spend a good part of it in undevitalizing action. Ageing is thus discouraged explicitly and encouraged implicitly by conditioning.

The person tries to cope with the drain on his life's resource. He remembers previous good times; has nostalgic reveries more real than the repetitions he is making. He gets stuck in nostalgia; one good time, the best time, its sights and sounds. He relives turning points, endlessly rearranging the drama to arrive at a different present. He leaps forward. Fortune, fabulous fortune, ridiculous abundance and its power to make a corner of the world his own in which he can work, or rest, himself into the ground.

The person's necessities are numbed. Their connections with constants are all but broken. Exploitation of constants left the person dumb. Conditioning of necessities leaves the person numb. Phantasies remain, perpetual childhood or adolescence; pictures of an acre of freedom. Only pictures remain. The person has learned obedience and how to disconnect from what is being learned. Breaking this connection snaps the links with constants. Words, work, art and belief have no place. They are troublesome now. Exploitation and conditioning are linked with an ever increasing scarcity. There is less for the person and less of him.

The dumb, numb person panics. There are still contradictions. From place through sex and purpose to destiny there are unresolved and unresolving conflicts. The dumb, numb person, the abnormal person, can go with senselessness so far. Giving up struggles, conforming regardless of the nature of the conditioned obedience, dislocates the person from contradictions but does not remove them. For the person always reacts and does not act. He has the rewards but they bring comfort not joy. The rewards make conformity easier. The person has a little bit of security. But the security is stultifying his contradictory problematic of movement and rest, change and stasis.

The rewards remove the person from the front line of exploitation and conditioning. His fear is of returning to being pulled or pushed back into exposure. He does not want to be seen. He does not want to see the front line clearly. He does not want those now in the first line to move. He wants them to stay there; he wants them to bear the rage of his contradictions. After all they represent his contradictions in freer form. He projects in panic. He panics and projects. They

— the first line — are threatening me. He threatens them back. He baits them, he batters them. He urges others to condemn those vociferous in their contradictions. He discharges his tensions momentarily and returns to feed his frustration on them once more. He will sacrifice others in attacking their contradictions. The person panics; projects; sacrifices others and sacrifices his panics and projections. The person is weary but must go on. His contradictions must appear to be outside him to have nothing to do with him; to be the property of a person condemned for his contradictions. The person translates terror into horror; terrified he hurls his horrified abnormality at struggling normality. The person sickens and wearies. His contradictions remain; he must resolve at least some of them. But he has lost contact. His constants were left skeletal by exploitation, his necessities were confused by conditioning. His contradictions are left hopeless. He does not have the equipment to tackle all of them nor can his contradictions revive themselves. The person falls asleep. Warm and wretched, alive, dumb, numb and dull. The person has completed a career without cause and with wholly personal effect the person has been abnormal and is now a vegetable. No day matters, all days are the same. The fears are dim, all the senses for relating to problems and potentials are blunted. The vegetable person's death is opportune at any time.

    Two themes thread through this process. The person is getting more like an object in himself and to himself; and the person's first reaction to exploitation, conditioning and projection is fear. The more power is exercized over the person the more power is taken from him. The more he is moved around or held still the more he is distressed at becoming an object. He is out of the plans and yet a part of the action. He is being directed and produced as a person. He is a cipher and a metaphor to himself. He struggles and finds that the extension of power is force, that force is threat, violence against him; pain and suffering. He is as frightened

71 Some thoughts which may be obvious

to leave being an object as he is fearful being an object.

Fear is not a reaction to power nor is it what is observed. Fear is attributed to persons in *cul-de-sac* confrontations. The person is at a dead end. What is observed has, however, all the signs of ingenuity of the person's awareness. The person pleads; hides; busies about doing nothing; talks without listening; listens without talking and overcomes these clear signs with hypocrisy. Hypocrisy is saying one thing and meaning another; withholding a meaning and conveying one calculated to have a particular beneficial effect to the person. A mask goes up. A thought made and an expression conveyed, none of which need bear any relationship to each other. Intention and impression are concealed whilst a particular view and a processed expression is conveyed. The person is double thinking. 'I'm in here; he can't see me. If I tell him so, so I can see him and find out about him. I won't let him know I've seen anything and I'll express agreement or ask for expansion to find out some more.' Co-operation is then disguised surveillance, conversation is an enterprise to avoid chance contact. Friendship is feigned and movements subverted. The person in hypocrisy, the abnormal person, has no company; company is a threatening swamp; he has no privacy: aloneness is cold loneliness. The hypocrisy reifies his contradictions with two further intentional contradictions: one within to expose others and conceal self and one outside to withdraw from others and to draw them on. Hypocrisy is a clear outcropping of fear. Thus fear pushes the person on and holds him further back: making panic and projection almost sensible reactions.

Abnormality, then, has two aspects. First, the warp, the hump, the person's problem with being exploited, conditioned and projected. Second, there is the person's efforts to normalize the warp, to bend it back to a less obvious significance whilst exploiting, conditioning and projecting.

That which makes the person abnormal, then, is a little complicated. It begins with the effect of exploitation of constants. Then comes conditioning of necessities. And it is furthered by projection of contradictions. Trialectic linkages are bombarded. The person allows and accommodates. The person is then getting by; really trying not to be noticed; hoping beyond hope that the accommodations work, believing in the accommodations more than the damaged perspectives they are to accommodate. The abnormal person defends his abnormality skilfully and purposefully. Abnormality is a position of so far and no further; the fear is of the next step, the big last step that makes the defences useless.

The abnormal person is not abnormal in the sense of mentally ill or mad. Madness has relevance; the mad person says what he sees, has all his perspectives and scrambles his actions and awareness in wholly personal experimentation. Abnormality is not gibbering euphoria, it is not the lunatic at full moon. The abnormal person means a defence of obsession; compulsion; fetishism; hysterically sensitive areas; needing a drug to survive; twisted and tortured digestion to a point of fiery insensitivity. What is abnormal is the all-importance of each of these defences in contrast to the unimportance of any of the facets of the perspectives. The person is abnormal because he must return time and again to an action which hides his fear and hurries it on to greater proportions. The abnormal person is in panic and ripe for projection. Projection is giving up even the few defences and going on the endless attack. Projection has no personal criteria; no particular preferences, no skill in its expression. Projection is kill — kill — kill; hate — hate — hate. Projection pounds away at the abnormal person; each blow outwards is a bruise within. The person is beating himself to senselessness, the person is beating away at senselessness, the person is beaten by senselessness. For beneath the vegetable person there is the dust person: the black hole fills in.

73 Some thoughts which may be obvious

Am I in any sense accounting for all of mental illness? I think not. Certainly not in the sense of accepting all existing classifications and attempting to give the diagnosis. Especially not in the sense of outlining the condition by specifying therapy. I am accounting for mental illness by saying what 'makes a person mad' and what if intensified and qualified; ramified, extended and interwoven in a sticky way, will keep him that way. Figuratively speaking the person gets so badly wounded so often that he is permanently sick. Theoretically it requires sustained and systematic exploitation, conditioning and projection to make the person abnormal and this process needs to be refined and tailored to him to make him a vegetable person. The abnormal and vegetable person are reversible states, the person being 'built-up' by the removal of exploitation, conditioning and projection and by sharing, learning and introspection.

7

Sociology in the light of the person

Which way are we facing? Towards subject-sociology perhaps?

Sociologists study people. The study is the art of accounting for social order amongst social beings. Yet a unit, the person, is an unknown in the structuring of known orders. There are people, we can agree. What then is a person? The family, the firm, the nation-state are all constructs and matters of ordinary perception. Each has both its known components with theoretical linkages and its everyday obviousness.

A dual order of thought is evident: there is the sociological map and the social terrain. But it is the landmarks of this terrain that are clearly problematic to sociology. The person is a non-entity in its reasoning and yet the maker and manifestation of all its arguments. Let us discuss the notion of the person in the context of current sociology. Let us try to reason what is making sociology unreasonable. Let us see that the inability to state who we are talking about inhibits us from knowing what we are talking about.

Parsons and Goffman agree on one thing: the person is an actor.[1] The actor has a part, a social face or script is his theatre of action. The actor is a being capable of learning his part, expressing his part and identifying with his part. Somehow he is separate from it and integrated with it. The actor-person is wide-open, willing and able. He does not exist until he has his part when he is a teacher, father and friend.

When he has these parts he is hard put to be anything else. The actor-person needs persona to express himself. His self is then subordinate to his persona and his persona is its means of expression.

No sociologist would say that people are merely the parts they play. Even those we call actors are also acknowledged as people who act for a living. And they give us a clue. Acting is not a means for a person to exist. It is a mode of subsistence with its mythology of potential success. An actor earns a wage and can by diligence increase this to a small fortune. The person inside, as it were, is pushing his part.

But Parsons and Goffman have no wish to pursue the actor to his self or his mind. The dramaturgical analogy thereby suits the stage but the offstage person, 'the whole being', is not credit worthy. And, of course, the whole being is an inadmissable element if people *are* merely players. It suggests an hypocrisy, a latent schizophrenia and, more parochially, it is the province of psychology. The person, then, figures in sociology impersonally putting on an act and lives in psychology recuperating, perhaps, from the drama. The persona is active and social whilst the person is inactive and private. There is a further clue in this bald axiom: the actor-person exists at large and the sub-person exists in solitude but again to pursue the problem is supposedly to leave sociology.

The person in sociology is thus pursued into a part and is not pursued when he vacates it. In the crudest of thought the person does not leave parts he changes clothes. The person is barely credited with the ability to dress himself.

This is not to say that sociologists do not think about people. In ordinary conversation sociologists are as glib as any other educated employee as to why they act and the motives of those around them. In fact, then, sociologists have private theories about people which ostensibly do not enter their public theorizing.[2] They can accept that people do things for money, power, status and a quiet life. They can

evaluate the performance of peers in these terms. These
private theories do, of course, inform public thinking by the
omissions and commissions in reasoning for social action. If
there is a need for order then each person needs order, is
averse to disorder and appreciates an order being given him.
Omitted are the many other perspectives a person may have
to novelty being created in and around him. But then this
sort of perspective is inadmissible and smacks of shallow
metaphysics. Public theories of sociologists are down-to-
earth; realistic if nothing else. The person has the range of
actions and reactions permissible within the paradigm of his
persona. If the persona is disturbed he is disturbed. The
disturbance is simultaneous and sympathetic to the point of
being identical.

I am proposing that this compartmentalization of theory:
that there are public theories about sociology and private
theories about people (and some people, types of people and
a person in particular) is the product of a gullible process that
involves believing the dramaturgical analogies prevalent in the
discipline and finding them useful in holding down a job. I
am further proposing the barriers be removed and that the
wealth of private theories sociologists have about people be
openly invested in the poverty-stricken public sociological
theory. I further propose that the recognition of the person as
a unit of analysis in sociology is a political act for sociologists
and that recognising the person as a unit of social action
entails a reconciliation of personal actions and social actions
in terms of being political actions.[3]

Nevertheless this is probably a premature attempt at a
sociological philosophy. For what I am trying to say is that
there is no future in the questions of what is the place of the
person in sociology or what is the fit of man in society. The
person, in my view, is stronger than any subject that studies
him and defies any simple juxtaposition with a single social
context. In contrast to the person sociology is at play. It does
not greatly affect the person what sociology says of him.

Sociology is, however, greatly affected by its assumption of innate imperfectibility: by its vision of the perverse person. An imperfect person needs watching and looking after. His 'whole' is not important because his behaviour is so cunningly errant. Parsons's phrases on actors convey a dazed being stumbling along dimly perceived tracks who, when wakeful, becomes avaricious and dedicated to having yet another fling in the bushes. I said at the beginning that this depiction says far more about sociologists than about the person. In terms of my understanding of abnormality, it is projection.

The problems of sociology become those of the containing of this wayward being. The question becomes how can you make the person's actions predictable? He does after all need looking after; what else does he need doing to him to get his being sorted out? Obviously all of the person's potentials are then represented solely as problems; change is made something the person fears and resists rather than makes; habits are clung to like Peanuts with his blanket. The person is a mess.

The group, the organization and the society are supposed to save the person from falling apart and from wrecking his situation as he wrecks himself. The sociologist colludes with these groups to get a grip on the person, to locate the person in an occupational category; programme the characteristics of that category; detect the bolt-holes and escape routes and plug them; pattern sanctions as socialization for miscreants and give the blue print to the administrators of occupational categories. Sociology is more interested in the principles of administrative control and ever less interested in what that administration is doing to those it controls.

It is commonplace that colluding with power structures constitutes a political act of mutual support and unilateral dictate. It is clear that the social sciences in this country are funded by 'practicality' and that this means administrative utility. It is important to realize the consequence of this condition upon knowledge. Sociology is being used in applied settings; hypothetical controls are produced; sociology's knowledge is of modes of control; there is no sociology left to apply.

The political act of sociology is in the values of sociology; in what is esteemed; in what sociologists work upon. The values of the subject are in the value put on its subjects. My argument is simple: unless the subject is given supreme value the study becomes active in the opposition to that subject. We do not judge the person's actions. The person can do neither right nor wrong. He is acting and creating, reacting and recreating. His behaviour is sensible because he is sensible. Administrative definitions of good and bad cannot be accepted nor notions of deviance.

To this extent subject-sociology is an apology for the person. Rebellion and movement do not distress sociology. Subject-sociology accepts the vitality of a change of heart.

Subject-sociology takes freedom as the axiomatic condition for considering the person and takes part of the responsibility of the realization of that freedom. That is, it gives back to the person what has been seen of him, its knowledge of the person is for the person. This represents the well-known fact that the sociologist is also studying himself; in learning about other persons the sociologist is learning about their constructions and reconstructions. He is simply a man who has talked with more men than most and has observed upon his observations to instruct himself in how to participate and how to observe.

The political act of subject-sociology is to work for that subject's completeness in terms of it being neither necessary or desirable to persons to have a sociology of themselves or being sociologists themselves.

Two political acts are entailed in subject-sociology then:

1 To assume freedom in and of the person and to observe inhibitions.
2 To relate inhibitions to the inhibited that they might be better equipped to free themselves from inhibitions and the knowing of inhibitions.

Subject-sociology starts by making man free in its discourse; continues by enabling freedom in men's intercourse and ends when sociologists are less than liberated persons in a situation of free consciousness.

Subject-sociology is drawn from three traditions, or apocalyptic visions, in the history of thought. First the enlightenment tradition of arguing from natural man; man with his political clothes off; man in the beginning and the determination from the beginning of man. In a sense this is the most obvious place to start. The person is the nature of man and the nature of the person. The person is not innately perfectible; the person is perfect *now*.

Second there is a thread from oriental and specifically Zen-Buddhist thought; of the infinity of paradoxes in which the soul is trapped until freely ensnared. The love of life above all, all life being sacred, no life ever being sought or taken. The domination of nature being the biggest problem; how do you respect that which you can control? Self-discipline, self-mastery; the end of egoism; the love of God in everything and of everything; the aspiration of mysticism; the search for the light of the seer. Love as law; the beauty of all. Life in abundance *now*.

Third there is the wrack of Marxist thought. The grim horror of oppression; the insanity of alienation; the timeless trap of exploitation and the immanence of the overthrow of the small minority of dedicated exploiters. The death of life in a multitude of forms, the joy of consciousness and of carrying life forwards or backwards in imagined realities. The withering away of deadening regimes and their escalation of torture. Not as they wither away, the whittling away of the state *now*.

These three threads are an intellectual legacy that carry the intellectual deep into thinking about life. They are the moving forces of thinking clearly about current situations that contain the thoughts as the person moves through their realms. Subject-sociology is about rehumanizing sociology to some

purpose. The purpose is to put the person back into its
equations; to equate the person with life and to propose that
the person has life more abundantly. Subject-sociology is
not accumulative, it is intentionally auto-destructive. The
liberation of the person, the lending of thoughts to
consciousness, is a task worthy of sociologists, worth doing
and liable to liberate sociologists.[4]

Sociology is an attempt to answer the question who are they?
Who is controlling what happens: who is breathing life and
death into the living? Quite simply which persons own and
control other persons? Sociology names names; identifies
logic of networks of owners and controllers by the
relationships between them. Sociology is an eye for the near
blind. Sociology cuts through the fog; the make-believe; the
bad dream to what is real in making fog; feeding phantasy
and giving nightmares. Sociology is thoroughly partisan; it is
an arm of understanding.

Subject-sociology is a further and final break with the
technological nonsense of post-war functionalism and
positivism; a child of the critical generation (the 1900s in
European thought) and an end to the amazing assumption
that sociology is only responsible to its sponsors.

Further subject-sociology needs no occupational niche; no
career escalator; no masters and slaves; no experts and no
professional associations. It recognises that if the problem,
perspective and person enquiring are clear then so is the likely
expression. Sociology is easy in its problems but its modes of
answering them have become an impossible maze. Most stand
at the entrance collecting fees, admiring the few that return
having rested on the bench in the middle. Mazes are for
passing time, sharpening the memory, being single-minded
enough to solve a puzzle. Subject-sociology is for seizing time,
sharpening the imagination, being multi-minded enough to
blow the game.

Quite obviously the tilting at objectivity is over. No more criticisms of method are needed. As the proper study of man is man, the ontology is more pressing than the epistemology. A theory of being should rise up within sociology and seize what it really has to say: how being regarded as different people licenses being treated as different persons; sociology can outline the divisive forces in social life without arguing any false, soporific unity.

Objectivity is about integrity. Integrity is only safe in action.

⑤

I suggest that those trained in the last century of struggling with subject matter down through concepts, collect their theories and go to work with the persons in whom they still have an interest; become as one and re-personalize themselves. Sociologist does not mean a person employed as one it means a person doing something sociological. If sociologist has come to mean primarily an occupational label then it is a product of occupational ideology in the context of a prevailing ideology of occupations.

Again what I am saying is that the job is to illuminate persons to persons as a person. It is a wholly and solely humanistic task. To measure some persons for other persons as a non-person is a wholly anti-humanistic practice. There is, however, one additional investment to be made for all this effort: the sociologist is looking at what is happening to get in between that and what will happen. The sociologist is taking the person seriously. If he is creative he is normal, if he is repetitive he is abnormal. The person has it in him. What is stopping it getting out? How long can a person be bottled up without blowing up? Can the person get back together after an explosion of frustration?

All I have said rests upon a few basic themes. Do sociologists care about the future as much as they care about their own?

Do they seek to escape from their recommendations for the control of lives of other persons? Could the sociologist benefit from being on the receiving end and would the benefit be to his giving?

Enough has been learned in the last century about social structures as theoretical and practical problems. Since Marx, through Weber past Durkheim the structures have shown consistencies. Structures are supportive and stultifying; progressive and regressive; monolithic machines and multitudinous tapestries of social relations; containing and constraining. Structures give dominance, command duty; get obedience and are given loyalty. The person is in love with the structure he hates. He hates thinking about it but what would he think about if it wasn't there for him? If anarchy is necessary to the construct of the person is it necessary to the person? But is that asking each person to give up the little bit of security they have got and walk off into the void? Will the sociologist go too?

The arguments on perspectives; on the theory of the person, on abnormality and now on sociology when confronted with the person have made great use of the ideas, the truths, of space and time, and their surfacing in change. These are true properties of the person, of his making and of his redefining. The concept of the person is most able to approach these, the realities of reality, and yet be the idea that contains them. The person is man, mankind in sociology and for sociological purposes. A purpose for sociology is the continuous liberation of the person and the liberation of sociology by people.

Annotations

'Nowadays men everywhere seek to know where they stand, where they may be going and what — if anything — they can do about the present as history and the future as responsibility. Such questions as these no one can answer once and for all. Every period provides its own answer. But just now, for us, there is a difficulty. We are now at the ending of an epoch and we have got to work out our own answers.'

Mills (1971 ed.:183-4)

1 Sighting the person

1 'Had we a science with the courage and authority to concern itself with mankind, instead of with the mere mechanism of vital phenomena, had we something of the nature of an anthropology, or a psychology, these matters of fact [suicide] would be familiar to every one.'

Hesse (1966 ed.:59)

2 Cf. Heidegger (1967) esp. 306-12.
'phenomenology is our way of access to what is to be the theme of ontology, and it is our way of giving it demonstrative precision. *Only as phenomenology, is ontology possible.* In the phenomenological conception of "Phenomenon" what one has in mind as that which shows itself is the Being of entities, its meaning, its modifications and derivatives.'

(1967:308)

3 Cf. Coulson and Riddell (1970).
'Human beings have an almost unlimited number of characteristics, and we are able to analyse them sociologically because everyone shares some characteristics with others as well as having some different ones, which they probably share with someone else. It is the *total* combination which is unique, not every individual characteristic. Thus in rational terms, human individuality, uniqueness is no barrier to sociological explanation. Since an individual does not respond to a situation in terms of discrete characteristics, but as a whole person, it is clear that the actual prediction of an individual's behaviour in a situation is a much more difficult job than making general predictions about the likelihood of behaviour occurring in certain groups under certain conditions.'

(1970:24)

4 'The sociological form of the "stranger" reveals Simmel's (1950) love of the paradox by emphasizing a mixture of opposites — complete liberation and absolute fixation . . . a person may be *in* the group but not of it.'

McLemore (1970:86)

5 Mills (1971 ed.:192-5)
'Freedom is, first of all, the chance to formulate the available choices to argue over them — and then the opportunity to choose.'

(1971 ed.:193)

6 'Absolute essential Being is therefore, not exhausted by the characteristic of being the simple essence of thought; it is all actuality, and this actuality exists merely as knowledge. What consciousness did not know would have no sense and can be no power in its life. Into its self-consciousness knowing will, all objectivity, the whole world, has withdrawn. It is absolutely free in that it knows its freedom; and just this very knowledge of its freedom is its substance, its purpose, its sole and only content.'

Hegel (1910 ed.:614)

7 'Buddhism, though based on falsehood, gathered round it, as it grew, a most lovely morality and a breadth and poetry in its theory of the origin of all things, which I do not think we find in the more positive theology of Christianity. It guarded as sacred the Great Mystery and that is the reason, I believe, of its charm to modern thinkers.'
Webb (1971:108)

2 A theory of the person

1 'From this concept of dynamic relatedness it follows that for Marx "the wealthy man is at the same time one who *needs* a complex of human manifestations of life, and whose own self-realization exists as an inner necessity, a *need.*" Hence "poverty is a passive bond which leads man to experience a need for the greatest wealth, the *other* person person".'
Fromm (1968:11)

2 'The man in me would do almost anything.'
Dylan (1970)

3 'There is normally a graduated scale of motives, by which men from different social classes are driven to work. Whenever a man rises to a higher class, from unskilled labourer to skilled labourer, from small tradesman to large-scale entrepreneur, from petty officialdom to a learned profession, once in the ranks of the élite he switches over from one set of motives to another.'
Mannheim (1940:316)

4 'When the spring comes, a young fresh life will show itself over the whitened sepulchres of the feeble generations which will have disappeared in the explosion. For the age of senile there will be substituted a juvenile barbarity, full of disconnected forces. A savage and fresh vigour will invade the young breasts of new peoples. Then will commence a new cycle of events and a new volume of universal history. The future belongs to Socialist ideas.'
Herzen, quoted in Aldred (1933:41)

5 'Would it not be necessary?' ... 'No, thrice no! ye young romanticists: it would not be necessary! But it is very probable that things may *end* thus, that *ye* may end thus, namely "comforted" as it is written, in spite of all self-discipline to earnestness and terror; metaphysically comforted, in short, as Romanticists are wont to end as *Christians.*'

Nietzsche (1909:14)

6 'Nevertheless I adhere to the perspective that each part is an emphasis and not a conceptually distinct part. Thus I have eschewed "saying it all".'

Lévi-Strauss (1966:152). The 'totemic operator' 'The whole set thus constitutes a sort of conceptual apparatus which filters unity through multiplicity, multiplicity through unity, diversity through identity and identity through diversity. Endowed with a theoretically unlimited extension on its median level it contracts (or expands) into pure comprehension at its two extreme vertices, but in symmetrically reverse forms, and not without undergoing a sort of tension.'

Lévi-Strauss (1966:153)

3 The cup of constants

1 'And it is indeed this transcendental consciousness which constitutes our empirical consciousness, our consciousness "in the world", our consciousness with its psychic and psychosocial *me.*'

Sartre (1967:327)

2 Tilgher (1930, ch.1).

3 'Kuhn (1970) argues "that there are periods of normal science in between which are scientific revolutions". He says that instead of one development simply being added on to another, the scientific revolution replaces one time-honoured scientific theory with another essentially incompatible with the older theory.'

Urry (1973)

87 Annotations

4 'This ended, the dark plain trembled so mightily, that the memory of the terror even now bathes me with sweat. The tearful land gave forth a wind that flashed a vermilion light which vanquished every sense of mine and I fell as a man whom slumber seizes.'
Dante (1891 ed.:15)

5 'Hindsight is always 20/20, but never more than when the owner thinks he is scanning with the lenses of historical determinism.'
Loizos (1970:114)

6 'Self-observation aims primarily at an inner self-transformation. Man reflects about himself and his actions mostly for the sake of remoulding or transforming himself more radically. Normally man's attention is directed not towards himself but towards the things he wishes to manipulate, to change and to form. He usually does not observe how he himself functions. He lives in immediate acts of experience; he is absorbed in them without ordinarily comprehending them. He reflects and sees himself for the first time when he fails to carry through some projected action and as a result of this failure is thrown, so to speak, back upon himself.'
Mannheim (1940:57)

7 'Love moved me, and makes me speak.'
Dante (1891 ed.:8)

8 The meaning and metaphor 'orgasm' is a direct usage of Reich's (1969) work. Particular emphasis has been made of a climactic rhythm and its undulating closure.

4 *The plain of contradictions*

1 'The purpose of this study is to approach the problem of human life with the assumption that man's social belonging, social participation on the one hand, and his

solitariness, his cut-off-ness on the other, are central issues and not derivative symptoms.'

Halmos (1952:15)

2 'People say we got it made, Don't they know we're so afraid.'

Isolation, Lennon (1972)

3 Characteristically humour is seen as man's *response* to tragedy. Clear writing in this vein can be found in Mailer (1970:56), Heinlein (1969:287 - 90), Chesterton (1940:35) and Hesse (1966:207). I would suggest, following Nietzsche (1909) that the Apollonian and Dionysian 'spirits' are in embattled contradiction.

5 *The wheels of the life-cycle*

1 Watson (1968:202).

2 'The epoch is an act of withdrawal from the usual assertiveness of consciousness regarding what does and does not exist in the world. The effect of this withdrawal is to reveal the world as a correlate of consciousness.'

Sartre (1967: n.4, translator's note)

3 See especially Goodman (1970:introduction).

4 The idealism of 'perfection' is at its most clear when in dealing with the fate of a movement, it is mandatory to catalogue the cruel repressions it must withstand to survive and the violence it must embrace to succeed.

6 *Some thoughts which may be obvious*

1 I do not deny the heuristic value but I doubt the value of 'heuristicism'.

2 And yet 'communal analyses' have been as comparably weak. Shanin (1976:361).

3 This section is keenly dependent upon advice from Mick Bloor who thought that a theory must cope with its own deviance and Geoff Pearson who showed me how 'anti-psychitriatic' analyses paid scant attention to the patient's actual illness. For example Scheff (1966).

7 Sociology in the light of the person

1 'While Parsons' voluntarism places great importance on man's efforts to realize certain ends, it is paradoxically true that these ends are no longer seen as derived from him; though they reside *in* him, they derive *from* social systems. Man is a hollowed out, empty being filled with substance only by society. Man thus is seen as an entirely *social* being, and the possibility of conflict between man and society is thereby reduced.'

Gouldner (1969:206)

'Goffman's image of social life is not of firm, well-bound social structures, but rather of a loosely stranded, criss-crossing swaying catwalk along which men dart precariously. In this view, people are acrobatic actors and gamesmen who have, somehow, become disengaged from social structures and are growing detached even from culturally standardized roles.'

Gouldner (1969:379)

2 'In this way sociologists' "troubles" are sociological "issues" if the practitioners have the requisite courage.'

Mills (1971 ed.:14-15)

3 'If he is so enlightened, he may begin to identify himself with that which liberates as well as that which orders. He might, in fact, go so far as to render unto the natural sciences the bondage to order that is theirs and unto the

social the dialectical transcendence that lies implicit within social research.'

Friedrichs (1972:271)

4 'This is a basic issue . . . and it claims the attention of the entire profession: how can we continue to believe that changes may be produced by an educational system, or other action programme, when our own best evidence demonstrates such efforts seldom produce significant change?'

Gaff (1973:553)

Bibliography

Aldred, G. (1933), *Bakunin*, Strickland Press, Glasgow.
Castaneda, Carlos (1968), *The Teachings of Don Juan: A Yaqui Way of Knowledge*, Penguin, Harmondsworth.
Chesterton, G.K. (1904), *Napoleon of Notting Hill*, Bodley Head, London.
Coulson, M., and Riddell, D. (1970), *Approaching Sociology: A Critical Introduction*, Routledge & Kegan Paul, London.
Dante Alighieri (1891), ed. *The Divine Comedy*, trans, C.E. Norton, Houghton Mifflin, Cambridge, Mass.
Dylan, B. (1970), *New Morning*, CBS Records, London.
France, R.T. (1970), *The Living God*, Inter-Varsity Press, London.
Frankfurt Institute for Social Research (1956), *Aspects of Sociology*, with a preface by M. Horkheimer and T. Adorno, trans. J. Viertel, Heinemann, London.
Friedrichs, R.A. (1972), 'Dialectical sociology', *British Journal of Sociology*, vol. 12, no. 3, 263 - 74.
Fromm, E. (1942), *The Fear of Freedom*, Routledge & Kegan Paul, London.
Fromm, E. (1968), 'Marx's contribution to the knowledge of man', *Social Science Information*, vol. 7, no. 3, 7 - 17.
Gaff, J.G. (1973), Review, *Contemporary Sociology*, vol. 2, no. 5, 551-3.
Gerth, H.H. and Mills, C.W. (1954), *Character and Social Structure: the Social Psychology of Institutions*, Routledge & Kegan Paul, London.
Goodman, M. (1970), *The Movement Towards a New America*, Knopf, New York.
Gouldner, A.W. (1969), *The Coming Crisis in Western Sociology*, Heinemann, London.
Halmos, P. (1952), *Solitude and Privacy: A Study of Social Isolation*, Routledge & Kegan Paul, London.
Hampden - Turner, C. (1971), *Radical Man*, Doubleday, New York.

Hegel, G.W.F. (1910), ed, *The Phenomenology of Mind*, trans, J.B. Baillie, Allen & Unwin, London.
Heidegger, M. (1967), 'Phenomenology and fundamental ontology', in *Phenomenology*, ed. J. Kockelmans, Anchor, New York. Extract from M. Heidegger, (1962), *Being and Time*, trans. J. Macquarrie and E. Robinson, Harper & Row, New York.
Heinlein, R.A. (1969), *Stranger in a Strange Land*, New English Library, London.
Hesse, H. (1966 ed.) *Steppenwolf*, Penguin, Harmondsworth.
Kuhn, T.S. (1970, 1962), *The Structure of Scientific Revolutions*, University of Chicago Press.
Laing, R.D. (1960), *The Divided Self*, Penguin, Harmondsworth.
Laing, R.D. (1967), *The Politics of Experience and Bird of Paradise*, Penguin, Harmondsworth.
Lehman, E.W. (1973), Review of 'Reflections on the causes of human misery and upon certain proposals to eliminate them', by Barrington Moore, Jnr, *Contemporary Sociology*, vol. 2, no. 5, 468 - 73.
Lennon, J. (1972), *Imagine*, Apple Records, London.
Levi-Strauss, C. (1966), *The Savage Mind*, Weidenfeld & Nicolson, London.
Loizos, P. (1970), Review, *British Journal of Sociology*, vol. 21, no.1, 114 - 15.
McLemore, S.D. (1970), 'Simmel's "stranger": a critique of the concept', *Pacific Sociological Review*, vol. 13, no. 2, 86 - 94.
Mailer, N. (1970), *Why Are We in Vietnam?*, Panther, London.
Mannheim, K. (1940), *Man in Society*, trans. by E. Shils, Routledge & Kegan Paul, London.
Mills, C.W. (1971 ed.) *The Sociological Imagination*, Penguin, Harmondsworth.
Mukerjee, R. (1961), *The Philosophy of Social Science*, Macmillan, London.
Nietzsche, F. (1909), *The Birth of Tragedy: or Hellenism and Pessimism*, trans. by W.A. Haussmann, Foulis, London.
Reich, W.R. (1969), *The Functions of the Orgasm*, Panther, London.
Sartre, J.P. (1945), *Existentialism and Humanism*, Methuen, London.
Sartre, J.P. (1967), 'The transcendence of the ego', repr. in *Phenomenology*, ed. J. Kockelmans, Anchor, New York, pp. 324 - 38.
Scheff, T.J. (1966), *Becoming Mentally Ill: A Sociological Theory*, Aldine, New York.
Shanin, T. (1972), Units of sociological analysis', *Sociology*, vol. 16, no. 3, 351 - 67.
Simmel, G. (1950), 'The stranger', in *The Sociology of Georg Simmel*, trans. K. Wolff, Free Press, Chicago, pp. 402 - 6.
Theodorson, C.A., and Theodorson A.G. (1970), *A Modern Dictionary of Sociology*, Methuen, London.

Tilgher, A. (1930), 'Work: what it has meant to men through the ages',
trans. from *Homo Faber*, by D. C. Fisher, Harcourt, Brace, New York.
Urry, J. (1973), 'Thomas S. Kuhn as sociologist of knowledge',
British Journal of Sociology, vol. 24, no. 4, 462 - 73.
Watson, J.D. (1968), *The Double Helix: A Personal Account of the
Discovery of the Structure of D.N.A.*, Weidenfeld & Nicolson, London.
Webb, B. (1971), *My Apprenticeship*, Penguin, Harmondsworth.
Weil, S. (1952), *The Need for Roots: Prelude to a Declaration of Duties
Towards Mankind*, Routledge & Kegan Paul, London.